Rainbows in Coal Country

Carole Harris Barton

PublishAmerica
Baltimore

First printing

ISBN: 1-4137-4897-X
PUBLISHED BY PUBLISHAMERICA, LLLP
www.publishamerica.com
Baltimore

Printed in the United States of America

for
my brother John
and
my daughter Noelle

Acknowledgments

This book did not spring eagerly into the light of the present, but rather, meandered unhurriedly out of the shadows of the past. Many people made its journey possible. For professional and institutional assistance, I am especially appreciative of: Carl Boone, Manager, Western Kentucky District, Mine Safety and Health Administration, U.S. Department of Labor; J. Steve Gardner, www.miningusa and Engineering Consulting Services, Inc., Lexington, Kentucky; Dennis McCully, West Kentucky Representative, Kentucky Coal Council and Harold Utley, President, Historical Society of Hopkins County (Kentucky), who generously shared with me their knowledge and research resources; and the good people at PublishAmerica, who do their painstakingly glorious work so well and with such consideration for their authors.

For personal support, I am indebted to:

My brother, John, who lived many of these events with me and helped me fill in the blanks when my memory couldn't;

My pastor, Dr. James F. Hoffman, Jr., who encouraged me to begin this work, and Nancy Smithers Bowles, who encouraged me to continue it;

Victor Dymowski, Melba Gandy, Bob and Sue Lotz, and Morgan Sisk Watley, who read excerpts and told me not just what they liked but why they liked it;

Beth Hayworth MacClaren, who read every word of my first draft and laughed in the right places, and Gretchen W. Harris, who read every word of my final draft and cried in the right places;

The women of Fairfax Baptist Church in Fairfax, Virginia, and Skycrest United Methodist Church in Clearwater, Florida, who listened with rapt attention as I read excerpts in their hearing; and last if not least,

My husband, Paul, who understood the creative process and knew when to leave me alone and when not to.

To all these helpers I am deeply grateful. You improve my work, but more than that, you enrich my life. Thank you, my colleagues, friends, and loved ones.

Word from the Author

When I began this work, my sole purpose was to introduce my daughter to the coal country of my childhood, a world of places she had never experienced—a rural home, a one-room schoolhouse, a coal mine, a country church, a country store. But during the writing, the little girl who lived these events seized my heartstrings and laced them throughout my motley collection of tales, weaving them into a patchwork of life as rich in human spirit as was the land in natural resources. And when I finished, the places were merely a backdrop for the people, all of whom, except for family members, I have given fictitious names: teachers who taught the facts, preachers who preached the Word, and children who learned from both; family members who valued kinship, neighbors who practiced friendship, and parents who lived the truth in selflessness, courage and moral integrity.

We can never do great things, said Mother Teresa, only small things with great love. This is my small thing.

Table of Contents

One. Rainbow Hope

Two. Rainbow Tears

One. Rainbow Hope

The rainbow of hope suspends
and the river of rapture flows . . .[1]

– William Sharp

Rainbow in the Cedar Chest -- I

We eyed the cedar chest. We had grown up together; he knew when not to look his younger sister in the eye and I knew when not to say a word. Faced with a chore that neither of us wanted, now was one of those times.

Okay, John, here goes. Bending down, I turned the key in the lock. *Mother and her keepsakes! She couldn't say goodbye any more than Daddy could, she just had a more socially acceptable way of showing it.*

It was a disagreeable task, closing Mother's apartment and moving her into a nursing home where she could be safe despite the Alzheimer's disease that every day cruelly snatched another bit of her fragile mind from her frail body. Daddy had died 10 years earlier. One moment he was installing playground equipment at the church; the next moment he was gone. Felled unexpectedly by his first heart attack, it was a fitting passage. The man who never said goodbye didn't have to.

They overcame so much. But how? How did they never give up? Never give up, never give up . . . the words swirled in my mind like fallen leaves in the wind, whirling, spinning, turning. *Never give up, never give up . . .* Suddenly, time pivoted and I was a child again. Standing with young parents outside our modest rural home in west Kentucky coal country, I heard their voices, felt the wet grass on my bare feet, remembered the day the rain retreated, the sun surfaced and the rainbow rose like a prayer to heaven.

Unaware earlier that morning of the splendor outside, a cardboard box raising me high enough in my chair to reach the table, I had sat idly in my nightgown, one index finger pushing around in my cereal bowl the last straggling milk-drenched cornflake. The screen door squeaked.

Bounding inside, his wet tracks following him on the worn linoleum-covered kitchen floor, Daddy let the rickety door slam behind him. "Let me show you somethin', Carole Sue," he said eagerly, picking me up and carrying me outside. Mother was close on our heels.

The last of the rain spilled off the ragged edges of our gutterless roof and splashed into the furrow near the foundation of the house, spattering mud onto the red brick pillar underpinnings and filling the air with the smell of damp earth. Standing me in the wet grass, Daddy squatted at my side, stretched out an arm and pointed to the sky. "See the rainbow? I don't think you've ever seen one."

At first, I didn't see it. Then suddenly, like an optical illusion transforming itself, the sky dropped its cloak and the rainbow burst like a river of rapture on my sight. Its curve rising above the tree line along the dirt road in front of the house, the striped pink and yellow arch soared upward and suspended itself against the blue, where its wispy tail faded into nothingness.

Spellbound, I dared not look away, as though my gaze glued to the ascendant arch would bond it to the sky forever. Like Thoreau, who once stood at the abutment of a rainbow as it cast a tinge on the grass around him, I was dazzled.

"You gotta have rain before you can have a rainbow," said Daddy.

"And it's God who makes the rainbow," explained Mother. Then she told how, a long time ago, a man named Noah built a big boat to save himself, his family and a boatload of animals from a world flooded in a rainstorm. And just when Noah and all the people on the boat were about to give up hope that the rain would stop, it *did* stop, and God set a rainbow in the sky as a sign of His promise that He would never again let a flood destroy the world. After that, every time Noah saw a rainbow in the sky, he knew a change for the better was on the way.

"So a rainbow is a sign of hope," said Daddy.

"Uh-huh," nodded Mother. "No matter how bad the storm gets, it will always stop and the sun will come out. So never give up hope. Because if you give up hope, you give up."

On a summer morning in the 1940s, I locked the rainbow in my memory bank; on an autumn evening in the 1990s, I unlocked the rainbow in the cedar chest. And down the slope of the heavenly arch slid the towheaded child who once I was, adventurous and ready to explore. Like Niagara's elfin rainbows skipping in the spray from rock to rock, she skipped in my mind from memory to memory.

My muse, my light, my guide, she took me by the hand. And drew me deeply into the coal country of my heart.

The Ones Who Lived

They told it for the first time in the year they put the baby in my dress and laid him in the ground. They told it for the last time in the year we put Daddy in his suit and laid him beside the baby. Even then, decades later, they seemed to like telling the story as much I liked hearing it. Like this time.

"See that little yellow house up there, Carole Sue?" Mother asked, nodding toward the open field. "That's where you were born." Kneeling on the seat by the car window, I stretched my neck, pressed my nose against the glass and gazed beyond the passing parade of fence posts.

Dilapidated and abandoned, the once lively house sat vacant and forlorn, its missing front door a victim of vandals, its drooping front porch a victim of time. With its sagging foundation now incongruously anchored in a golden sea of wheat, the forsaken derelict looked out its shattered front windows toward Highway 85 as it stretched west across the gently rolling hills to Madisonville, the county seat of Hopkins County and the heart of the west Kentucky coalfields.

We were on our way there, Daddy driving, Mother beside him, John and I in our usual places in the back seat of our old Chevy. The little yellow house was now disappearing from view, if not from Mother's thoughts. "Your daddy and I moved there after we left your Grandma Harris's house, where we lived when we first got married. Your daddy's mama was good to us, but—"

Mother had a way of not finishing her sentences, but I knew what she meant because of the other times she had told me. Had she finished, she would have said that she and Daddy had wanted their own place, so they saved their money so they could buy furniture and move out of Grandma's house.

"That little yellow house wasn't much," continued Mother, "but it was everything we had hoped for. We painted on the mailbox, 'Sterlin' and Mary Harris.' We were proud!"

But I was ready for the next part of the story, the part about me. "How come John was born in the hospital and I was born at home?" I knew the story about my year-older brother's birth and mine, but I wanted to hear it again.

"Because I was sick when John was born," Mother said, throwing him a glance. "Toxemia, the doctor said. I was in a coma and didn't even know when they took me to the hospital, much less when John was born. I'm lucky to be alive—John, too—the doctor says."

"Uh-huh." I could see Daddy's eyes searching for me in the rear view mirror as he switched from John's birth to mine. "The night you were born, it was rainin' cats and dogs, I mean a real gully washer. We didn't have a car then, and I had to leave your Aunt Peggy with your mother while I walked the whole eight miles to Madisonville to get the doctor. That night, I walked past several stalled cars drowned out by the heavy rain. And when I got to the doctor's house, I was soakin' wet."

"Then what happened?"

"Then I got in the doctor's car with him and he brought me back to the little yellow house."

It was Mother's turn again. "When you were born, your navel cord was wrapped around your neck, your face was all puffy and your lips were so swollen that they were turned almost inside out. I thought the doctor would never get you to breathe, and when you finally did, you squalled bloody murder and I thought you'd never stop," she chuckled. "It was pretty fightenin'. But you lived, you and John. Y'all were the ones who lived."

I didn't ask any questions about the one who didn't. I knew I wasn't supposed to, and anyway, I remembered. But if they didn't volunteer—and they usually did—I asked for my birth story every time we passed by the little yellow house in the golden sea of wheat. No matter how many times I heard it, it was never too many.

The first time, it told me I was important. The last time, it told me they were.

Gum Balls and Disagreements

The bumpy gravel road turned south off Highway 85 at the Pond River Collieries sign about seven miles east of Madisonville. Meandering across country a mile or so, the rutted road angled east at the big elm, where a narrow offshoot arced around the massive tree and continued south. A few hundred yards down the offshoot road past the spreading limbs of the well-known local landmark, a dirt lane turned up a grassy hill to the Wagner house, known by the surname of the property owners. My first remembered residence, it was the house we moved into after leaving the little yellow house.

Crossing a shallow creek spanned by a wooden bridge of partially loose planks that rattled and groaned underneath the weight of the car, the lane leading to the Wagner house was often littered with sweet gum balls. Thorny, woody and inedible, the spiky seed balls had once hung like bristly brown nuts from the limbs of an overhanging sweet gum tree. I well remember those burr-like balls about an inch in diameter, having once stepped on one barefooted. The experience stuck the memory in my four-year-old mind as surely as the gum ball stuck in my foot.

"We've got a tree like that," said Miz Lily one day, her small birdlike hands nervously flitting up to tuck behind her ears the unruly wisps of dark gray-streaked hair that seemed always to escape, no matter how often she smoothed them back into place. Mother busied herself in the kitchen while our closest neighbor chattered, the tip of her tongue occasionally reaching out to brush the purplish pea-sized protrusion on her upper lip as she spoke of her husband. "I tell Ed not to drive over them silly little ol' gum balls. They'll bust the tires out."

"Oh, really?" Mother raised her eyebrows.

That night, Mother told Daddy about the visit. "Lily was here today. A big cloud came up, and you know how scared she is of thunderstorms. She was knockin' on our front door before even a single raindrop hit the ground."

"Is that so?" Daddy yawned behind *The Madisonville Messenger.*

"Lily says she won't let Ed drive over them silly little ol' gum balls. She says they'll bust the tires out."

"Uh-huh."

"Bust the tires out, my hind foot. That Lily! I don't know what in the world she's thinkin'. Them gum balls won't bust out nothin'. Lily's so dumb!"

"No," said Daddy offhandedly. "She's just a worrier."

18

Mother said dumb, Daddy said worrier. I was confused about Miz Lily, but I wasn't confused about Mother and Daddy. They had a disagreement.

It wasn't much of a disagreement, nothing at all like the biggest one they would ever have, the one that would come years later and awaken John and me during the night to fill our hearts with fear.

But this disagreement, the one about Miz Lily, was like most of their other disagreements: a little prickly, but harmless. Like the gum balls.

Four Rooms and a Path

Daddy's blue eyes looked into the white-framed rectangular mirror hanging over the washstand in the kitchen. Well into his morning routine, he was shaving off his reddish whiskers. Occasionally pausing to swish his razor in the water-filled washbasin beside the bucket of drinking water and its aluminum dipper, he ran his hand over the smoothness of his bald head. It was as though he might surprise himself someday and find growing there some of the strawberry blond hair that had started falling out during his early twenties.

The Wagner house was a real version of the proverbial four-rooms-and-a-path. Without electricity, automatic heat or running water, the plain white frame house was a simple square divided into two rooms across the front and two rooms across the back with a path leading to the outhouse, just like in rural folklore.

I remember nothing in the living room except the old upright piano, its dark finish crackled and its ivories yellowed with age. "It was my daddy's piano, and when your daddy and I got married, Daddy gave it to me," Mother told me with pride. "But I think my daddy was really givin' it to yours." For although it was a Sisk piano, it was a Harris who played it.

A self-taught musician who never learned to read music, Daddy had a natural gift, and his fingers knew just where to touch the keys to coax out the music that silently lurked inside. The magical instrument and its companion claw-footed swivel stool enthralled John and me, but the piano wasn't a toy, Mother cautioned, the warning in her eyes enough to keep tiny fingers away from the keys.

Besides four wooden chairs and a rough handmade table passed down from Grandma Harris, the kitchen housed a coal-burning range and a stand-alone cabinet for dishes and cookware. Adjacent to the kitchen was John's and my room, furnished with a few wooden chairs and the metal double bed where John and I slept.

But the most interesting room in the house was Mother and Daddy's bedroom. Its main features were Mother's mirrored dressing table with its backless bench, her locked cedar chest and the only wall art in the house. "What's that?" I asked one day, pointing to the gold-framed document, its beautifully flowing calligraphy flanked on each side by a delicate pastel watercolor of a bluebird holding a pink ribbon in its beak.

"Your Daddy's and my marriage certificate," answered Mother. "I decided to get it out of the cedar chest and frame it." The symbolism of the certificate's presence on the wall above the headboard of the bed was lost on me, even if the importance Mother gave it was not.

In this four-rooms-and-a-path were my first memories formed, my concept of family shaped, my view of the world framed. In this four-rooms-and-a-path were no problems and no trouble.

But life changes, and so do perceptions. And by next year, I would become intimately acquainted with trouble.

Bluegrass Bedtime

Daddy reached for his fiddle. *Oh, Daddy's gonna play for us.* The four of us had gathered by the light of a kerosene lamp in the bedroom John and I shared, Mother busy with her latest needlework project.

Daddy sometimes spent the evening cleaning and polishing his hunting rifles and shotguns, but tonight, it was fiddling time. I loved the bluegrass tunes he played, a more frequent expression of his untrained musical ear than was playing Mother's beloved piano.

"Play 'Pop Goes the Weasel,' Daddy," John begged. It was a novelty, because when Daddy got to the "pop" part, he would take his bow off the instrument and pluck the string with his finger to make a popping sound.

"No, Daddy," I countered. "I like the one that sounds like a choo-choo." I could almost see the train roaring down the tracks when Daddy slid his fingers up the fingerboard to make the high whistle sounds—whoo, whoo, who-OOO-ooo—and slid them back down the lower strings to make the gliding double stops of the coarse, grating CHUG-ga chug chug, CHUG-ga chug chug of the engine.

Mother was the mediator. "Play 'em both, Sterlin'," she said. "Play 'Pop Goes the Weasel' and 'The Orange Blossom Special.' And then play 'Ol' Joe Clark.' He washed his face in a fryin' pan and combed his hair with a wagon wheel." *Combed his hair with a wagon wheel?* In the mind's eye of this young literalist, the nonsensical image was too much. *You can't comb your hair with a wagon wheel; it's too big! And anyway, it's round.*

"Well, at least he had hair," joked Daddy. Then, sitting ramrod straight, he tucked the fiddle underneath his chin and began to play, dipping and swaying as the music overtook his body, one foot tapping the floor to the beat of the music. Transitioning to a different key as needed, he skillfully wove one tune into another, occasionally stopping to rub a little rosin on the hair of the bow or to adjust the pitch of a string by slightly turning a peg. More tunes in his repertoire than we had named, Daddy played and played, filling our ears with melody.

Too soon, bedtime was upon us. Carefully, Daddy laid his instrument in its felt-lined case and unscrewed the knob that loosened the horsehair in the bow. Sliding it through the loops that secured the bow inside the lid of the black carrying case, he closed the lid, latched it and set the case in the corner.

After they listened to our prayers and tucked John and me into bed, Mother picked up the kerosene lamp. "Call me if you need anything," she said. Carrying the lamp, she followed Daddy into the adjoining bedroom, leaving the door slightly ajar so she could hear us if we called.

A faint shaft of light slipped stealthily through the opening, highlighting the cracks in the bare floor and forming a perfect backdrop for the soft murmur on the other side of the door. Muted parental voices in the dark of night, the comforting hum of John's and my bluegrass bedtime.

It was our only lullaby. And the only one we needed.

Secrets and Treasures

Mother was dressing for a trip to Madisonville, the special preparations demanding my full attention. I stood at the side of her dressing table.

"I sure am glad the freckles on my face aren't as dark as the ones on my arms," she sighed. Then, fluffing powder onto her face, she rouged her cheeks and brushed her auburn-tinged dark hair. "When I was a kid, my hair was redder than it is now, and Earl and Leonard called me 'Red-on-the-Head.' I would get spittin' mad, which is why they said it, of course. But I didn't know that at the time," she laughed, recalling the teasing of her two older brothers.

Preoccupied, Mother still managed to notice as I fingered the pastel green hairbrush, comb and mirror resting on top of the dressing table. "Your daddy gave me that dresser set," she said. *Ooo, Daddy gives Mother really pretty things!*

"Mary's vanity things," Daddy said from his place at the door. He was dressed and ready to go, one hand clutching his felt fedora, the other hand grasping the doorknob. Always ready to leave before Mother was, especially if it wasn't a dress-up occasion when he needed her help to knot his tie, he stood at the door waiting, his hand on the doorknob a not so subtle attempt to hurry her along.

Opening a dresser drawer to deposit her rouge and powder inside, Mother selected a lipstick and dropped it into her purse. "I'll put my lipstick on in the car," she said, in an obvious response to Daddy's silent impatience.

My eyes, now riveted to the treasures inside the drawer, took in the full array: a bottle of perfume shaped like a heart, a golden tube of lipstick and a black-enameled one, a bottle of red nail polish, and now the tiny pot of rouge and the round pink box of face powder with its fluffy pink powder puff. Marvelous things, unattainable things and inaccessible, they were woman-things, things a little girl could only hope for in a future so far away that it seemed like never.

But as special as was the dressing table, it paled in comparison to Mother's intriguingly mysterious cedar chest. My access to it was infrequent and short, and although she wouldn't allow me to touch anything inside it, she on rare occasions allowed me to look at what she removed and showed to me.

"It's *my* cedar chest," she would say. "Your daddy gave it to me when we got married." *Oh, when you get married, your husband gives you a present.* "All my most important things are in here.

Nobody gets to see inside my cedar chest unless I say." Then she would lower the lid and turn the key in the lock—click!—before I could get more than a glimpse inside.

And she said the exact same thing every time she opened the cedar chest, as though I would forget. But I would never forget. The cedar chest held far too much mystery, far too many hidden secrets and imaginary treasures for me ever to forget.

I would never forget. Never.

Hard Water

Gingerly dipping my fingers into the white enamel bucket Daddy had filled with water from the well, I lightly smoothed the wetness between my thumb and fingers. *It doesn't feel hard to me.* Then I shook a few drops into my upturned palm. *It's not. It's not hard!*

I didn't know what to think. Well water was hard and rainwater was soft, Mother and Miz Lily said. But I had already tested the water in the rain barrel, and it felt just like the well water.

Eventually, I would understand. In coal country, all well water was hard, so high in mineral content that skin washed in it felt tacky to the touch until dry, and clothes washed in it dried thick and stiff. But all I knew at the time was that water for laundry came from the rain barrel Daddy had placed underneath the eaves of the house, and water for drinking, cooking and bathing came from the well at the end of the lane strewn with sweet gum balls.

"Bet I can beat you to the well," I challenged Daddy on our daily trek to draw water. We often enjoyed a footrace to the well, and I always won.

"Bet you can't," he replied, accepting my dare. "Go!" We started running, Daddy swinging an empty water bucket in each hand. Laughing, his eyes sparkling, he reached the well a step or two before I did. I laughed, too, because I thought I was supposed to. But I didn't really feel like laughing.

I was still smarting from the defeat when we started back to the house with the water. "Bet I can beat you to the house," I challenged a second time.

"Bet you can't!" And we started running again, Daddy carefully balancing the full buckets so the water wouldn't slosh out on the ground. This time, I reached the goal ahead of him. "You beat me, you beat me!" he exclaimed, setting the buckets on the edge of the porch and plunking himself down beside them. And this time, he wasn't laughing.

Daddy's not laughin'. Why isn't Daddy laughin'? Suddenly, I realized the race hadn't been fair. Daddy had carried two full buckets of water, but I had carried none. *Daddy's sad that he didn't win. I didn't mean to make Daddy sad. It must be the hard water; I bet it's really heavy. I bet Daddy could have won if the hard water wasn't so heavy!*

This stocky and very muscular young man, this strong man fit from daily manual labor in the coal mine, this athlete who played catcher on the community baseball team—this is the man who lost a footrace to a four-year-old. Right! But at the time, I had no perspective on daddies and little girls in competition with one another, only a child's sense of fair play and a developing sense of empathy. And so great a misunderstanding about hard water that I never again challenged Daddy to a footrace on the trip from the well, only to it.

It wasn't generosity; it was self-protection. I couldn't bear to see Daddy sad.

Ribbon Bows

Uncle Mason walked through Grandma and Grandpa Sisk's living room with three-year-old Betty Sue perched on his shoulders. Her brown braids tied with pink ribbon bows, she was more dressed up than usual.

I liked Uncle Mason, Mother's youngest brother. He had a ready laugh and he looked a lot like her, except that he was bigger. Sometimes he held me on his lap, Betty Sue on one knee and me on the other.

Grandma had just served a big meal in her kitchen. The house was full of relatives and neighbors, so many that there were not enough chairs to seat everyone and some people sat outside on the porch steps or stood in the yard. Everybody was talking about which car to ride in and with whom. I sat on Mother's lap and watched.

Betty Sue had ribbon bows in her hair and I didn't. Every time Mother put ribbon bows in my hair, I got to go somewhere special. *Betty Sue's gonna get to go and I'm not!* Even at four, age has its privileges. "How come Betty Sue gets to go and I don't?" I whined.

"Because it's her mother," answered mine.

I had started to protest when a woman with outstretched arms approached Uncle Mason. "Poor little thing," said the woman, reaching up to retrieve Betty Sue from his shoulders. "She don't even know her mama's dead. Nobody knew Cornell was havin' trouble with the baby; we just knew she was expectin'. And then when she got sick, it was just like that," she said, snapping her fingers, "and she was gone. It's such a shame, her so young and all. And the baby dead, too."

Tsk Tsk Tsk, went the woman's tongue against her teeth, every tiny tap imprinting the picture in my mind like a tinsmith hammering metal: Betty Sue in pink ribbon bows on the way to her mother's funeral.

I would carry the image forever, an indelible mental tattoo.

Child Labor

Play is a child's work. And like our parents, John and I were hard workers. Sometimes we dumped dried beans into a metal stew pot and capped it with a lid, then sat on the floor underneath the kitchen table shaking the pot up and down to hear the metallic rattle the beans made. And sometimes, pretending a big corrugated cardboard box was our car, we took turns sitting in the box and pushing each other around the kitchen. "Ooga, ooga," we squealed, imitating the sound of a car horn.

Another time, in a supreme act of disobedience, we gleefully jumped up and down on our bed to see who could bounce higher. But when John caught his head underneath my chin and bounced me off onto the floor, the resulting crash brought Mother charging into the room wearing her angry face. "You kids stop that, right this minute!" she demanded. We already had.

We had dolls, too. My Mary Jane wore a print dress of tiny blue flowers on a field of white, and John's Overall Bill wore denim bib overalls over a light blue chambray shirt, just like the ones Daddy wore to the coal mine. But Overall Bill's cap was not at all like Daddy's. Overall Bill wore a soft cap of narrow blue and white stripes, not a protective hard cap like Daddy wore. "Overall Bill's a railroad engineer. He drives a train," said Daddy.

"I'm gonna be a railroad engineer and drive a train when I grow up," said John, dreaming the dream of a man-child.

But my favorite game was dress-up, a game for just Mother and me. Adorning me with one of her necklaces and a pair of earrings, she smoothed lipstick on my mouth while I held the green-backed mirror from her dresser set and watched my lips change from pale pink to bright red. After patting a little rouge on my cheeks, she dipped her fluffy pink powder puff into her box of powder and dusted some on my nose. I loved the powder; it smelled just like Mother smelled when she got all dressed up to go somewhere.

Leading me to the closet, she took her pastel blue dress from its hanger, saying the words she would repeat many times in the future under different circumstances. "You look pretty in blue; it lights up your blond hair and blue eyes." Then she reached for one of her hats and a pair of high-heeled shoes. When she buttoned the blue dress on me, tying the skirt up with a belt so the hem didn't drag the floor as I walked, I thought I was very special, and when she put the hat on my head, I knew I was. And when I walked—clack! clack!—the high heels clattered on the floor as little feet wobbled around the room in shoes I could barely keep on, Mother smiling as I paraded up and down.

Someday I'll be a real grownup woman, and I'll wear lipstick and high heels and smell good, just like Mother.

We were just playing, or at least Mother was. I was hoping.

Two. Rainbow Tears

Now welcome, welcome baby boy...
To the rainbow of their tears...[2]

— Padraic Colim

Waiting My Turn

John stood on the front porch of the Parham house in his new clothes and new shoes, his dark hair freshly combed. "My little man's all ready for his first day of school," beamed Mother, adjusting John's collar. It was her final inspection before the eventful departure.

The first day of school was very important, not just because it was the first day, but because now that John was in the first grade, Mother had let him abandon his short pants for long ones. She had called him her little man and he surely felt like one, standing straight and tall, obviously excited.

Mr. Parham had moved his family into Madisonville and turned over his land to a strip mine, and Daddy had rented the house. To get there from the Wagner place, we went to the big elm and traveled east, then took the south fork of the road at Miz Bessie's small grocery store. Going on past the mining camp and the access road to Pine Hill coal mine, we crossed the railroad and went past Wilson school. Just barely out of sight of the school and beyond a curve sat the house on the east side of the road.

Mr. Parham was a dish-faced man with sun-wrinkled skin and twinkly eyes who came regularly to the farm to care for the few horses and cows he kept there, but we seldom saw him. It was a good arrangement. The mine got the coal, Mr. Parham got paid for the coal and for renting us his house, and we lived close enough to Wilson school for John to walk there.

Mother and Daddy had talked about Wilson school ever since we moved into the Parham house. We would supply water to the school from our cistern—two of the older boys would come from the school every day with buckets to fetch the water—and we would provide room and board to the teacher, Miss Mary Jane. Very pretty Miss Mary Jane, with her long dark hair, tiny waist and brightly colored dresses, would eat and sleep at our house during the week, but would spend the weekends with her parents in Madisonville.

"'Bye, Daddy," said John as he and Mother stepped off the porch. "Be a good baby," replied Daddy. *He didn't say 'bye. How come he didn't say 'bye?* But it was no more than a passing thought that took second place to one more pressing: John was going to school and I wasn't.

Mother had said I had to wait until next year, but I didn't know waiting would be so hard. It wasn't fair! I was always allowed to go where John went, and I was as big as he was. But many things Mother made us do didn't seem fair, and we still had to do them; it wasn't as though we were allowed to choose.

"You just wait your turn," Mother called back to me, taking John's hand as they neared the road. "Next year you'll be six, and then you can go, too."

But a year is a terribly long time to wait when you're five years old, and occasionally, Mother dressed me up in one of my Sunday school dresses and let me walk to school with Miss Mary Jane and John. I was the center of attention from the older girls when we got there, and I loved every minute of it.

I wasn't very good at waiting my turn. Neither was Mother.

Trash to Treasure

The white frame Parham house was prettier than the Wagner house, more architecturally interesting with more and bigger rooms. Like the Wagner house, it had no modern conveniences. But the front door, which featured a vertical oval glass window, opened into a wide entrance hall, at the end of which was a door to a screened-in side porch. Off one side of the entrance hall was a door to the living room, and off the other side were three doors: one to Mother and Daddy's bedroom, one to John's and mine, and one to Miss Mary Jane's.

Adjacent to the living room was the kitchen, its back door opening to a screened-in back porch. Up against the wall in the corner of the back porch sat a white wooden icebox, underneath it resting a flat oblong pan to catch the leaking water from the slowly melting ice stored inside. Abandoned by the Parhams when they moved to Madisonville and into a house with an electric refrigerator, the icebox was ours by happenstance, an unexpected benefit of the move.

On ice delivery day twice a week, Mother placed in the front living room window a white cardboard sign bearing a large black number to signal the iceman the amount of ice she wanted to buy that day: 25, 50, 75 or 100 pounds. Spotting Mother's sign in the window—50 pounds was the largest amount our small icebox would hold—the iceman stopped his truck, walked around to the rear and unlatched the insulated door. Retrieving a large industrial-sized set of metal tongs, he grabbed a pre-weighed block of ice and lugged the dripping chunk around to the back porch. By the time he got there, Mother had propped the screen door open and was waiting beside the icebox to help him slide his burden inside before one more drip spilled wastefully on the floor.

From discard to discovery the icebox journeyed, and it moved not an inch; from useless to priceless, and it cost us not a cent. It wasn't just a matter of perspective, it was a matter of reality: one person's trash is another person's treasure.

Making Papers, Making Breaks

"'Bye, Daddy," John and I said in unison. Daddy had opened the car door and stepped out onto the street.

"Be good babies. I'll be back before you know it." *He did it again. He didn't say 'bye back to us.*

By now, I was shivering. It was just like the other nights that winter when we all went to Madisonville. Mother, John and I sat outside in the car while Daddy went inside a big building on West Center Street and stayed too long. "Daddy's goin' to school to make papers," Mother said.

You mean grown people go to school? "What kinda papers?"

"A certificate, proof that he learned what he's studyin'." *So that's why Daddy's been layin' out a bunch of books on the kitchen table after supper and sittin' there by the lamp readin' and writin' stuff down on paper.*

"He's learnin' about different kinds of gas and stuff, and how to ventilate the mine, and how much air the mine needs for a certain size room, and how much force it takes to send the air a certain distance," said Mother. *There are rooms in a mine?* "When Daddy finishes, he'll know a lot about minin', and if he passes the test at the end of school, he'll get papers. Then he can get a better job and we can start savin' money to get a house here in Madisonville so y'all can go to good schools."

Grandpa Harris had died when Daddy was 11, the next to the youngest of nine children. By all accounts, Grandma had a rough time keeping the family together, and she proved it once by forgetting to tell Daddy that she was moving the family to another house in the community that day. When he came home from school and found the house empty, he simply walked up the road to the nearest neighbor and asked if anybody knew where his mother was. Fortunately, everybody knew where everybody else was in that small rural area.

"Ma'am thought one of the older kids had told me we were movin'," Daddy laughed, referring to Grandma Harris by the unusual name that he and all of his siblings called their mother.

With no father to support the family, Daddy had gone to work in the mine when he was 14. "I looked older than I was," Daddy said. "I was shavin' by the time I was 13." But after he had worked a few weeks, the foreman found out that Daddy was underage for work and sent him home. Two years later he went back to the mine, and except during the Great Depression when the mine had shut down, he had been there ever since.

"Not everybody who takes the course passes the test," Mother told John and me weeks later. "But Daddy passed it on the very first try!" Then she took the certificate he had earned and locked it inside the cedar chest.

Neither Mother nor Daddy knew what Voltaire said, but they knew what Voltaire knew. People who don't get the breaks have to make their own.

Good as a Man

I sat on the floor in the living room gazing at the fireplace. *Green bricks are ugly.* To me, the decorative tiles surrounding the fireplace were bricks, considerably smaller and of a different color than typical bricks, but otherwise like the ones on the outside of expensive houses and buildings in Madisonville.

The living room fireplace was an exact replica of the one in Mother and Daddy's bedroom. Inlaid around their faces with glossy pastel green rectangular tiles, the coal-burning fireplaces showed off mantles of dark walnut like the woodwork in the rest of the house. Above the mantles spanned wide mirrors set between round wooden columns capped with ornately carved horizontal crosspieces that effectively framed the mirrors.

"I like this woodwork better than white," Mother had said when we moved into the Parham house. "Dark woodwork doesn't show as much dirt as white." Anyone who has burned coal for heat knows exactly what she meant. Each spring, after extinguishing the last fire in the open fireplaces, Mother washed the woodwork to rid it of the sticky, sooty film that collected during winter.

I didn't care about the woodwork, but no one who knows me now will be surprised to learn that, even before I knew what an interior decorator was, I dreamed of how to make our house look prettier inside. And without a doubt, the fireplaces would have been prettier if their decorative tiles had been pink, like Mother's powder puff. I knew all my colors and carefully chose them to make the pictures in my coloring books look pretty. *Wonder if. . .*

Suddenly inspired, I grabbed my pink crayon.

It wasn't going very well, I had decided, even before Mother discovered me at work. "Well, Carole Sue!" she declared, interrupting the tuneless whistle that often marked her routine work. "What in the world do you think you're doin'?" Expounding on the virtues of using a thing for its intended purpose, she confiscated my crayon before impounding the entire boxful.

Together, we scrubbed the pink crayon marks off the tiles, Mother interrupting her whistling again. "Ya' know, they say, 'A whistlin' woman and a crowin' hen/often come to some bad end.' I say nonsense! Some man made that up, tryin' to make a woman think he's better'n her. Why in the world shouldn't a woman do anything she's capable of? The very idea! I can whistle good as any man— better'n most." Mother was working herself into a tizzy, scrubbing harder and faster, her words growing more intense the more she thought about the injustice. "A woman is as good as a man, and don't you *ever* forget it!" *Okay, okay.*

"Now, promise me you'll use 'em only in your colorin' books," she said, calming down as we finished our work, "and you can have your crayons back." I promised, of course, and Mother resumed her whistling. She kept her word about the crayons, too, and so did I.

And decades later, when the women's liberation movement arrived, I already knew: A woman is as good as a man.

Love Stories

"You kids learn to say the Ten Commandments and the Lord's Prayer by heart," Daddy said, "and I'll get you your very own Bibles."

Sometimes he said the words for John and me, and sometimes Mother said them, giving us just a phrase and waiting for us to repeat it before giving us the next phrase. We learned the words by rote, and we had earned our own small Bibles before we could read. So significant were these gifts that I would one day wrap mine in white satin, cover it with fragrant white freesia and carry it for my wedding bouquet.

When Mother and Daddy were children, public secondary schools were in towns, not in rural areas—at least in that part of Kentucky. With no public transportation for rural students and no other way for Mother and Daddy to get to Madisonville, they had finished only the eighth grade.

Although their education was limited, their appreciation for it was not, and they told John and me that every day, both in words and actions. They praised school, admired teachers, talked about how they liked going to school when they were kids and bought books for us, instilling in us a love of learning. We had books of nursery rhymes and traditional children's stories: *Peter Rabbit, Little Red Riding Hood, The Three Little Pigs, Jack and the Beanstalk,*

Snow White and the Seven Dwarfs, Goldilocks and the Three Bears, and a book of Bible stories, one for each day in the year.

Every night before they put us to bed, either Mother or Daddy read to us, the other parent sitting quietly and listening along with us. More than the stories, I enjoyed sitting in their laps, John and I taking turns in the lap of the reader every other night. "Now," said the reader when it was time, and the child in the lap of the reader reached out and turned the page.

And sometimes in the morning while Mother made breakfast in the kitchen, John and I crawled into bed with Daddy. Pulling us close to his side and cradling one of us in each arm, he told us stories until Mother called us to the table. "Once upon a time . . ." he always began, telling us one of the stories from the books, the magical words carrying us far away to enchanted places, captivating places we had already visited in our imaginations but places deserving repeat visits. It didn't matter that we had heard the stories many times before. In fact, the better we knew them, the better we liked them.

It wasn't even about the stories. It was about the reassurance of ritual, the reliability of repetition, the sense of security in the private moments Daddy devoted only to us.

It was, in essence, about a man being a father. So mostly, it was about the love.

A Reindeer Christmas

"Get your coats on and come out here and see this," Mother said excitedly, pulling the bedcovers back for John and me. *Oh, goodie, Santa's been here!*

Our coats topping our pajamas, John and I stood in the front yard in our fuzzy slippers. "See?" said Mother, pointing to the ground, the brown grass dead and frost-crunchy beneath our feet. "See the tracks of Santa's reindeer?"

"Ooo," we exclaimed, the warm breath escaping our open mouths floating on cloudy puffs into the cold winter air. Amazing! Sure enough, the hoof prints were there in the ground, and I could almost see Santa and his sleigh.

Christmas was always too slow to arrive, the anticipation almost more than I could bear. I even had trouble falling to sleep at night. "Is Santa comin' to see you this year?" a woman at church asked me as our family walked up the steps to see the Baby who appeared every year in the Christmas play.

"Yes, Ma'am."

"Well, what will you do if he don't?"

You mean maybe he won't? I had never considered the possibility. "I guess I'd just about mitt ka-suicide."

Her riotous laughter told me I had made a mistake, but what was it? Bewilderment surely was written all over my face.

"It's okay, honey," said Mother, rescuing me. "We all know what you mean. Which is more than I can say for *some* people!" Glaring at the woman, Mother picked me up and carried me inside the church. "Of course, Santa Claus will come to see you," she soothed. "You have absolutely nothin' to worry about."

Even without electricity, our Christmas tree was festive, a wild cedar hung with decorative ornaments. Colored glass balls. Paper chains made of narrow strips of colored construction paper rolled into circles, linked and sealed together with glue. Fluffy white popcorn strung on Mother's crochet thread. Snowflakes cut out of lined notebook paper and strung on brightly colored yarn. Pinecones tipped with white paint and strung on metallic thread. Sweet gum balls coated with gold paint and tied by their stems to the tree branches with red ribbons.

The packages underneath the tree were the gifts we would give to other family members. Toys, books and items of needed clothing for John and me would be there only on Christmas morning after Santa had come the night before. *Mother and Daddy are just kiddin'. Even I know that Santa can't come down the chimney. It's too small, and anyway, the fire would burn his feet. He comes in through the door, just like we do. I'm the littlest, and they always try to fool me!*

Christmas Eve was a multiple holiday at our house, for it was Daddy's birthday and his and Mother's wedding anniversary. "Don't ever get married on a holiday," Mother would say decades later. "It makes the holiday too sad when one of you goes off and leaves the other." But that was a lesson she learned after Daddy died. Before that, the multiple celebrations called for multiple festivities.

After supper, Mother cut the homemade upside down pineapple cake that was Daddy's favorite: a yellow cake topped with pineapple wheels and caramelized brown sugar. Inside the holes of the pineapple wheels where other bakers sometimes placed candied cherries, Mother placed the tiny candles she lit just before presenting the cake to Daddy. After he made his wish, he took a deep breath, pursed his lips and began to blow.

John and I soon learned the game. Daddy never had enough breath, and at the very last moment, he motioned for us to help. Eagerly leaning forward, we huffed and puffed, all of us laughing when the last flame died.

Afterward, John and I gave Daddy the birthday present Mother had helped us select, and Daddy gave Mother a small gift. And so as not to confuse what we were celebrating, we obeyed two cardinal rules: never wrap Daddy's birthday present in Christmas paper, and never open Christmas gifts on Christmas Eve.

On Christmas Day itself, after we opened the packages Santa had brought, we went to visit Grandma and Grandpa Sisk, where all of

Mother's family gathered, the adults talking all at once during the major feast that Grandma served. John and I sat at a small separate table with Betty Sue and Doris Ann, Uncle Leonard and Aunt Madeline's only child, who was about John's age. Most of all, I enjoyed the fresh fruit bowl with sliced red grapes, orange sections and banana slices sprinkled with shredded coconut, a juicy indulgence that beat all to pieces the canned fruit cocktail we ate during the rest of the year.

But no other Christmas ever surpassed the one when Santa's reindeer left their hoofprints in the ground, even after John told me a year or so afterward what really happened. The barnyard gate had somehow come open during the night, and Mr. Parham's horses had escaped and trampled around the yard before Daddy caught them and put them back inside the fence.

It was a real shock. But not nearly enough to make a little girl just about mitt ka-suicide.

Woman's Work

Mother eyed the iron kettle leaning on its rim against a tree in the backyard, the morning sun still low in the sky. Finally resigned, she squared her shoulders, took a deep breath, picked up a basketful of Daddy's work clothes and strode down the back porch steps. Dropping the heavy basket onto the ground, she rolled the huge black kettle out from underneath the tree. Another day of woman's work had begun.

Carrying a galvanized washtub from the porch to the yard, she placed the tub beside the kettle and began the multiple trips to the rain barrel for the water she dumped by the bucketful into the containers. Butcher knife in one hand and a bar of homemade lye soap in the other, she shaved the soap into slivers, watching impassively as they fell into the kettle and began to dissolve.

Now it was time to start the fire. Collecting a bundle of downed tree branches, she inserted them underneath the kettle, splashing them with kerosene from a spouted metal can stored on the back porch. Tossing into the water Daddy's coal-blackened overalls and shirts, she pulled from her apron pocket a match and struck it against the kettle. As the air filled with the smell of burning sulfur, she backed off and flung the lighted match underneath the kettle. Flaring briefly, the flame waned, then began gently to lick the underside of the kettle.

Turning on her heel, Mother headed to the kitchen, where she built a fire in the range to heat a bucketful of water. Two galvanized washtubs on the kitchen table preceded more trips to the rain barrel, and by the time the last tub was almost full, the heated water was ready. Shielding her hands from the hot metal bucket with a quilted potholder, Mother poured the boiling water into one of the tubs and swirled the merging waters with her hand to create a warm mix. In went the family laundry and a wooden washboard, its front surface a series of smooth rounded metal ridges.

Stroking the washboard with a bar of laundry soap, Mother rubbed each item up and down against the soapy ridges, hand wrung the water out of the items and immersed them in the rinse tub. While the clothes soaked, she carried a cloth bag filled with wooden clothespins outside, where a rough wooden pole stood against the fence. "Gimme my laundry pole," said Mother to no one in particular, dropping the bag of clothespins onto the ground.

Grasping the pole with both hands, she stirred the clothes round and round inside the kettle until the boiling lye water flushed out the grimy coal dust. Then, using the rim of the kettle for leverage, she dipped the end of the pole underneath the clothes and lifted them, one piece at a time, out of the boiling water and draped them on a nearby bush to drip. When the clothes were cool enough to handle, she hand wrung them, tossed them into the rinse, sloshed them around, hand wrung them again and dropped them into the waiting basket.

"Thelma makes Floyd wear the same ol' dirty clothes to the mine every day for a week," Mother grumbled as though I weren't there. I almost wasn't. Mother was grouchy on washday and it was easy for me to get into trouble, so I made myself as invisible as possible and worked at staying out of the way.

Dousing the fire with the rinse water, Mother continued her self-chatter. "A man comes out of the mine dirty; he shouldn't have to go in it dirty."

Lugging the heavy basket and the bag of clothespins to the wire clothesline, Mother pinned the clothes on the wire while the kettle cooled. Then she upturned the kettle, rolled it back underneath the tree, turned it on its rim to drain and carried the empty tub back to the porch as she returned to the kitchen, where she finished the family laundry. When Daddy came home from the mine, he would help her carry the dirty water outside and dump it.

"Lord, please don't let it rain 'til my clothes get dry," pleaded Mother, occasionally casting a wary eye at the sky as she pinned the laundry onto the line.

"How come you keep lookin' up at the sky?" asked John. "I thought you asked God not to let it rain."

"Because I don't know yet what He's decided," she snapped.

Back inside, Mother smoothed lotion on her hands and dropped into a chair for a brief respite before starting supper. "If there's anything good about not havin' many clothes and only one change of sheets, it's havin' less wash to do."

After supper, Mother brought the dry laundry indoors and folded it into stacks. "I sure do dread ironin'," she said, brow wrinkled.

Drudgery to read about, woman's work was even worse to experience, and I can prove it. Mother never whistled on washday.

Never Done

In a house without electricity, Mother's iron really was iron: a heavy cast flatiron with a wooden handle on top. It took at least two irons to do the job—one to use and one to get ready for use. Rotating the irons on and off the hot kitchen range as needed, one iron was always heating as the one in use was cooling off. Mother usually had three or four irons going at once, all in various stages of readiness.

With no synthetic fabrics, all clothes and flat items had to be ironed, except for terrycloth towels, underwear, socks and bed linens. "I'm not ironin' these sheets," Mother had said when she removed them from the clothesline. "They smell better when they're fresh off the line, anyway. Irma says Ray won't sleep on unironed sheets. I say let Ray iron 'em, then! If Sterlin' Harris ever said that to me—"

I didn't know who Irma and Ray were, but I was certain Daddy was fortunate that he took no notice of whether his bed sheets were ironed or not.

Before ironing anything, however, Mother sprinkled it with water and rolled it inside a heavy towel to wait an hour or two while the dampness distributed itself evenly throughout the fabric.

When the clothes were ready, Mother picked up an iron and lightly spit on the hot soleplate to test it for the right temperature. If the spit hissed and bounced off in a droplet, the iron was hot enough; if the spit lay there in a flat sizzle, the iron was still too cool.

Padding the kitchen table with a folded quilt, Mother laid a damp item on the padding. First testing the underside of the item with the tip of the iron to be sure it wouldn't scorch the fabric, she pushed and pulled the iron back and forth across the unfolded damp item, smoothing out the wrinkles as the item dried.

On a hot summer day, the kitchen range going full blast to heat the irons, steam from the ironing table rose into Mother's face, reddening it and sending perspiration in rivulets down her cheeks to drip off her chin.

The very clothes on our backs and sheets on our beds the beginning of next week's laundry, it was woman's work. And it was never done.

Kentucky Fried Chicken

The soldiers were on the back porch, both of them dressed in khaki uniforms and wearing holstered handguns on their hips, just like in the pictures I had seen. Mother had opened the icebox to chip the ice she was dropping into the water glasses she had handed them. "No," she said. "I haven't seen anything unusual."

One of their comrades had gone AWOL, the soldiers said, and they were part of a search party from Fort Campbell, an Army fort straddling the Kentucky-Tennessee border about 50 miles away.

"What's 'AWOL'?" I asked.

"Absent Without Leave," answered one of the men. "One of our guys got homesick and sneaked off the base without permission, and we have to find him and bring him back." But the search had been fruitless, and the soldiers were heading back to Fort Campbell when they thought they heard a gunshot. It brought them in their Jeep to the house to see if everything was all right.

"Oh, that was just my little boy here shootin' off his toy cannon," said Mother, her hand resting on John's shoulder.

World War II was well under way, and military toys were common. John's cannon contained a lidded chamber into which he put a small amount of carbide, then poured in a few drops of water and closed the lid. Shortly, the gas built up inside the chamber and—boom! Such a thing could never make it past today's toy safety regulations, but Daddy had taught John how to use the toy and

Mother had insisted that he use it only outside. John had never had an accident.

"Y'all had anything to eat?" asked Mother. It was what Kentuckians do: offer food to guests, even unexpected ones, and even if there's a shortage of food.

"No, Ma'am."

"I've got some chickens. I can fry up a chicken, if y'all can wait for me to kill and dress it."

"Yes, Ma'am, we can wait," one of the soldiers answered, his eyes lighting up as he looked to his partner for concurrence. While Mother went about her business, another Jeep pulled up. "Uh..." the first soldiers hesitated, "can you take some more of us?"

"I've got lots of chickens," said Mother, heading to the backyard.

Soon more soldiers appeared, parking their Jeep in front of the house with the other Jeeps. Mother didn't say a word; she just headed out the back door to chase down another chicken. By the time she returned, another Jeep had appeared, then another. Back to the chicken yard again. When the last Jeep brought a gravelly-voiced older man with graying hair and a ruddy face, the sergeant in charge of the group, another chicken met its fate.

While Mother fried the chicken, the soldiers put John in one of the topless Jeeps and me in another and took us for a ride down the road and back. "I've got a little sister about your age," said the driver, giving me a glance. The breeze felt cool against my cheeks as I stood face forward in front of the passenger seat, the hands of the seated passenger anchoring me around the waist. I wished I could be in the Jeep with John, but Mother had given permission for us to ride in separate Jeeps, and I wasn't scared. Except a little.

When we got back to the house, the waiting soldiers were standing in the front yard smoking or sitting on the porch. Joking with one another, they teased the one they called Mis'sippi about his accent and said the one from Alabama was upset because Mother wasn't cooking possum.

46

"Don't tell my mom, Ma'am," said one of the soldiers after Mother took the fried chicken out to the front porch in big bowls, "but this is the best fried chicken I've ever tasted. What did you do to make it taste so good?"

"Usually, I soak it in salted water to make it tender, then give it a buttermilk bath before I roll it in the seasoned flour," she said. "Except this time, for lack of time, I just dipped it in the buttermilk. But these chickens were young, so they were pretty tender already. And I use lots of lard in the skillet, so the grease almost covers the chicken when I put it in. Then, just after it browns and right before I take it out of the skillet, I dot each piece with a dab of butter and let it melt and run down all over the crust."

"Sure is good!" said the soldier, hungrily biting into a drumstick.

I lost track of how many Jeeps came that day and how many chickens Mother fried, but there were fourteen soldiers, she told Daddy that night. "They were all real young, except for the sergeant. None of 'em asked for this awful war, they're all just somebody's sons." Then, a distant look in her eyes, she repeated it. "All of 'em— just somebody's sons."

An army moves forward on its stomach, it is said. I know it did that summer day—a stomach full of Kentucky fried chicken.

Coal Country Soldier

Mother was wearing a path in the living room floor with her repeated trips to the front window. It was time for the letter.

Pulling back the curtain, Mother looked anxiously down the road toward the school to see if Mr. Woodly was on his way. She knew what to look for: a rattling black coupe, older than any other in the community, the mail carrier positioned in the middle of the front seat rather than directly behind the steering wheel.

"Why does Mr. Woodly sit in the middle?" I once asked Daddy.

"I guess he got tired of slidin' back and forth across the seat from his mailbag on one side to the window on the other side to reach the mailbox." *Oh.*

As anxious as Mother was to get the letter, she didn't seem to want it. Still, when it came every month, she ripped it open eagerly. Knowing that the suspense would get to Mother while he was at the mine all day, Daddy had given her permission to open any of his mail from the local draft board.

The pattern was familiar. "Whew!" she would breathe, visibly relieved. "Daddy's been deferred again for 30 more days." Then she would take the letter and lock it in the cedar chest.

"What's 'deferred'?" I asked as she tucked the letter away this time.

"It means Daddy won't have to go to the war, at least not until—"

I knew about going to the war. Uncle Mason and Uncle Amplis, Mother's younger brothers, had already gone, and so had Daddy's younger brother, Uncle Lionel. Mother had showed me their pictures in their uniforms before she put the pictures in the cedar chest.

"Why don't Sterlin' have to go?" asked a woman at the grocery store one day.

"They need the miners to get the coal so they can run the war plants," said Mother. "Sterlin' is still doin' his part."

"Yeah, but he's not gettin' shot at!" snapped the woman, walking off in a huff. She had voiced the resentment felt by many people whose family members and loved ones risked their lives on the front lines while other able-bodied men stayed stateside, spared from war to make a different but necessary contribution to the war effort.

"Hands that dig coal are as important as hands that carry guns!" retorted Mother. But it was too late; the woman was gone. "Sterlin' answered the call of his country and he's doin' just what it asked him to, just like the others are," said Mother, determined to finish the conversation, if only with herself. "He's a soldier, too."

Mother had said it all. Daddy *was* a soldier—a coal country soldier.

Elephants in the Sky

Browder Methodist Church had no other rooms except the sanctuary, and in it, all church activities took place: preaching, singing, teaching, weddings, funerals—everything except eating. We ate at church only once or twice a summer, when all the women brought food from home and spread a potluck lunch on planks temporarily laid across wooden sawhorses outside underneath the trees.

The minister served four churches, preaching at each church once a month. "We get the preacher on the fifth Sunday once a year," said Mother, as though it were a privilege. I didn't know why; personally, I liked best the Sundays when he *didn't* come to our church. When he did, he went up behind the pulpit, yelled and stomped around and turned red in the face, and I got bored and couldn't be still enough to keep Mother happy.

But on the Sundays when the preacher wasn't there, we still put on our best clothes and went to Sunday school, where volunteers taught Bible classes. Mother had made for me two Sunday dresses and a white organdy pinafore, all three made without benefit of a sewing machine. "I made 'em on my fingers," Mother told one of the women at church. A sky blue dress and a cotton candy pink one, both with gathered skirts that peeked out from underneath the hem of the pinafore, made me feel almost as special on Sunday as I felt when Mother and I played dress-up.

John and I both wore lace-up high-topped shoes that Mother polished every Saturday night and placed on the living room hearth to wait until Sunday morning, but John's shoes were brown and mine were white. "Don't put your feet up under you when you sit down," Mother cautioned me. "The polish will rub off on your legs." Every time I forgot, I could see that she was right.

When the preacher wasn't there, Mr. Rob Crowe seemed to be the boss at church. He taught the men's class, and he stood on the platform up front with his hymnbook to announce the page number of the next congregational hymn.

The pianist had a hymnbook propped up on the music rack in front of her, and she looked at the book to know what notes to play—not like the way Daddy played without a book. "Sing out strong," Mr. Crowe shouted, his eyes peering over the top of his wire rimmed glasses as he occasionally waved his arms in the air to direct the congregational singing. Mother claimed she couldn't sing. But when the time came, she sang softly, almost underneath her breath, while Daddy sang out energetically. He had a good bass voice, I'd heard her say more than once. She was proud of Daddy; I knew it, even then.

The women's class was on the front two or three pews, and the children's class was on one of the back pews, which Daddy could see clearly from the choir loft where he sat in the men's class. If I talked too much, Daddy rolled up his Sunday school lesson guide, pointed it in my direction and raised one eyebrow. It was enough to put the fear of God in me, or at least to settle me down.

John and I sat on the back pew with the other children, our feet dangling above the floor. Miz Crowe was our teacher, and today's lesson was about Noah and the rainbow, the story that Mother and Daddy had already told me. But the story was more fun this time, because Miz Crowe gave each of us a colored cardboard picture of the ark floating on the floodwater and a sheet of paper containing small punch-out pictures of different animals in full color. We poked out the animal pictures, licked them on the back to activate the glue, and stuck the animals—monkeys, lions, birds, giraffes, elephants, zebras—onto the picture of the ark. There was no right or wrong place to glue the animals on the cardboard, Miz Crowe said; we could put them anywhere we wanted.

But not according to John, who already thought he was my boss when Mother and Daddy weren't around. "You can't put elephants up in the sky," John objected when he saw where I intended to place my elephant. "Birds go up in the sky, not elephants!"

"They're *pretend* elephants. They can go anywhere they wanna go!" And mine did—high up in the sky.

It was a sibling thing. John told me what to do and I did as I pleased. That way, we both got what we wanted.

Little Lamb

I had seen gravestones before, but this time, I noticed them.

It had been months since Mother broke the news to me in the kitchen. "You mean a real baby?" I was incredulous, playing with a piece of dough as Mother made biscuits.

"Yes," she smiled, twisting the cutter in the dough to form the biscuits before placing them in a bacon-greased jellyroll pan to slide into the oven. "We're gonna get a real baby, and we have to pick out a name for him." After that, the subject of names seemed to come up often.

"Maybe Dwight or Douglas," said Daddy one night at supper, calling the names of two well-known World War II heroes. "For General Eisenhower or General MacArthur. Or Jimmy, for General Doolittle."

"But I was thinkin' Samuel, for your first name. I just don't know!"

said Mother. I didn't know, either, and I don't remember any names for girls ever coming up.

One day while John was at school, Mother opened the cedar chest, took out an armload of items and separated them into stacks on her bed. "These are the baby's things," she said to me, taking an item from the top of a stack. Unfolding it, she held up a small white article. "See? This is a dress. It was yours when you were a baby." Then she refolded it and put it aside. Methodically, she repeated the process, going through all the stacks—gowns, blankets, crib sheets, diapers, undershirts—until she had told me the name of everything. Then, picking up the stacks one by one, she carefully placed them back in the cedar chest and closed the lid. Turning the key in the lock, she pocketed the key to return it to its hiding place. *The baby is really important if Mother keeps his things in the cedar chest.*

One night, a knock sounded on the front door, and when Daddy opened it, two men in white coats pushed a gurney into the hallway. *Who are these men? And what are they doin' with that bed on wheels?* Exchanging greetings with Daddy and following his lead, the men pushed the gurney into Mother and Daddy's bedroom. When they came out, Mother was lying on the gurney. "You kids go get your coats," said Daddy. "We're goin' with your mother to the hospital to get the baby." *Oh, I didn't know I was gonna get to go get the baby!*

Carrying Mother outside, the men slid transport and patient into an ambulance. *What kinda car is that with a door in the back?* "Y'all c'mon," said Daddy, hurrying John and me into the back seat of our old Chevy. "We're gonna follow 'em."

Standing on our tiptoes, John and I draped ourselves over the back of the front seat and leaned forward, trying to get closer to the ambulance as we raced down the road. "Get up closer, Daddy, so we can see Mother," we begged. Daddy seemed to be driving faster than usual, but the ambulance was throwing dust up into our headlights and we couldn't get close enough to see Mother. Faster and faster we seemed to go.

When we arrived at the hospital, Mother's sister met us in the lobby. *What's Aunt Peggy doin' here?*

"C'mon," said Aunt Peggy, taking John and me by the hand. "Y'all are goin' home with me." *Oh, goodie. I love to go to Aunt Peggy's.*

The next day, Daddy came to Aunt Peggy's house. Sinking heavily into a chair, he seemed different, even before I crawled up into his lap. "Did we get the baby, Daddy?"

"No," he answered quietly. And his voice sounded different, as though he almost couldn't say the words. "He was dead."

His tears came then, at first gently. But like a roller coaster on a downhill run, the salty streams gathered momentum as they raced down his cheeks, the pain inside him screaming for release. Great heaving sobs erupting from somewhere deep inside him, his body shaking, he clutched me so tightly that I thought he would squeeze the breath out of me. But I didn't say anything, because somehow, I knew not to.

Then Aunt Peggy came into the room, and she was crying, too. *Somethin' awful has happened when grown people cry.* And I cried because something awful had happened.

"When your mother comes home," sobbed Aunt Peggy, "you have to be really nice to her and be a really good girl." *I will, I will.*

At home another day shortly afterward, Daddy put on his navy blue suit with a white shirt and a tie. I always liked it when Daddy put on his suit, and Mother did, too. "Don't you look handsome!" she would say. She always smiled when she said it, fussing with his tie to neaten the knot and Daddy winking at her as she ran her fingers down his lapels. "You can't beat a Harris man—um, um, um! All the girls knew that, especially Emma Lu. First, she tried to get Joe," Mother would say, referring to one of Daddy's brothers. "Then, when Elizabeth got Joe, Emma Lu took out after you. But *I'm* the one who got you," she would laugh, giving Daddy a half turn, smoothing her hands across his shoulders and down his back. But this time, Mother wasn't there to fuss with Daddy's tie. This time, there was no flirtation, no intimate gesture for little eyes to see and young memories to record.

We always went somewhere special when Daddy had his suit on, and this time, we went to a big two-story house in Madisonville bigger than any house I'd ever seen, except from the outside. Many people were there: Grandpa and Grandma Sisk, Grandma Harris, all my aunts and uncles and cousins, Miz Lily and Mr. Edmund, Miz Bessie, and people I'd never seen before. Everybody talked in hushed tones.

"How's Mary?" someone asked.

"Still in the hospital," answered Daddy.

In one end of the room on a tall stand sat an open gray casket. *That big box looks a lot like Mother's cedar chest, except the cedar chest is wood.* Flowers surrounded the casket, baskets and sprays of flowers, more than I had ever seen before, their fragrance filling the air with a scent as pretty as they were.

"See, here's the baby," said Daddy, holding John and me up, one at a time, to see the baby lying in the casket. He was very still and white, not wiggly and pink like other babies I'd seen. *He's wearin' a dress from the cedar chest, the dress that used to be mine.*

A few days later, the ambulance came back to our house. Sliding the gurney out onto the ground, the men in white coats stood silently as John and I ran out the front door and climbed up onto the gurney to give Mother a hug. "You kids get off so they can carry your mother inside," instructed Daddy, after a moment. *How can Mother be cryin' and smilin', too?*

"No, it's okay," said the man with flaming red hair. "They aren't heavy." And the men gave John and me a ride when they picked up the gurney and carried Mother inside.

Days later, Daddy drove Mother, John and me to Bethlehem cemetery. "This way," said Daddy, leading us up the hill. "Don't step on the graves. It's disrespectful." *There are so many stones, and lots of 'em have angels and crosses and stuff on top!*

Soon we reached the right place, stopping in front of a tiny gray stone with the figure of a baby lamb lying on top. Daddy removed his hat, standing solemnly as Mother squatted on the ground. "Infant Harris," she read, tracing the letters on the stone with her fingers. *They're cryin'; be quiet, don't say a word.* I didn't, and no one else did, either, not even on the ride home.

They wept an invisible rainbow of tears for a long time after that. I know, because the tear denied by the eye is owned by the voice, and I heard tears in their voices every time we went back to visit the little baby lamb.

But I never again saw Daddy cry. Never ever again.

Three. Rainbow Beauty

... beauty will come to them in the rainbow ...[3]

–David Rosenthal

Roles and Goals

"What's that?" I pointed up the road from where John and I stood in our front yard.

"Road grader." *Oh.*

"What's it doin'?"

"Makin' the road better. Can't you see?" At age six, John was very knowledgeable. And very authoritative.

Yes, I could see, now that the big yellow machine driving down the road was closer to us. With its angled ground-level blade scraping the road and stirring up dust, the grader made horrendous noise as it evened out the ruts and smoothed down the bumps from winter. After the machine finished its work and moved on, a slow-moving truck dumped gravel on the road as men with rakes and shovels walked along behind, evenly spreading out the gravel.

"Engineers plan how to make roads," said Daddy that night at supper as he and Mother talked about the noticeable improvement in the road. "Engineers earn lotsa money. You've gotta go to college to be an engineer."

"I'm gonna go to college and be an engineer when I grow up," boasted John.

"Me, too," I chimed in, not to be outdone.

Mother shook her head. "Well, I don't know," she said. "You'll both go to high school, for sure. Your daddy and I will see to that. And when you do—you just wait and see—it'll be in Madisonville, where the schools are accredited." Mother was nothing if not dogmatic, stating an opinion as if it were a fact—for to her, it was. "But if there's money for anybody to go to college," she turned to look at me, "it'll be John. Because he'll have a family to take care of, and you'll have a husband to take care of you." *Oh.*

It was the prevailing view of the day, but what she said to me next was not. "But you'll still have to learn a trade or somethin', so you can get a job and take care of yourself if you ever have to."

Thus are roles assigned and goals set, in forgettable conversations on forgettable days forgotten by everyone. Or so you'd think.

Getting the War

Betty Sue was living with us now, except when she was with Grandma and Grandpa Sisk. "Poor little thing," Grandma Sisk lamented. "Her mama's dead and her daddy's gone off to fight the war. It don't seem fair."

"It happened, that's all," said Mother. "I think Mason was so lost when Cornell died that he didn't know what to do with himself. He's tryin' to outrun his hurt. Betty Sue can stay with us as long as she needs to, until Mason—"

But one day at Grandma Sisk's, I overheard Aunt Maxine and Grandma talking. With Uncle Amplis gone away to the war, his wife was often at Grandma's house when we were there. "Well, what if Mason don't come home?" worried Aunt Maxine. "Who'll take Betty Sue?"

"I don't know. Mary, I guess. She lost her last baby, ya'know. She's just not made for havin' babies. I don't think she'll try for another one. She almost died the last time." *I didn't know that!* "She's had three babies and not a single one of 'em a normal birth, not even Carole Sue's, with the cord wrapped around her neck and all. Mary's lucky she's got any kids."

"That's for sure."

"We all pray Mason don't get killed. But if he does, I think Mary will take Betty Sue, and I don't think she'll mind a bit."

I was beginning to get the war. I had thought it was bad because people had to go away. Now I knew it was bad because they might never come back.

Foreign Invaders

As much as World War II dominated the world scene, it was not the only war. Foreign invaders were destructive in the homeland, too.

One side of Uncle Ruel's body paralyzed from surgery to remove a tumor from his brain, Daddy's brother wouldn't make it through the summer—not because of the tumor, but because of the tuberculosis that had invaded his lungs years earlier.

A disease common to the U.S. in the early decades of the 1900s, TB had taken a huge toll on Daddy's family. Granddaddy Harris had died of it, and so had Daddy's oldest brother, Uncle Carmack. Another of Daddy's older brothers, Uncle Clarence, had spent several years in a tuberculosis sanatorium before he came out wan and emaciated. And a Navy physician had discovered healed lesions on Uncle Lionel's lungs before he went off to the war. "His body fought off the TB," said the doctor. "So he's safer from it now than he was before."

"You kids stay here. You can play in the yard. I don't want you goin' in the house," said Mother as she and Daddy stepped out of the car and headed down the hill to the ramshackle house where Uncle Ruel and Aunt Vivian lived.

"If we can't go in the house, how come John William and Jimmy can?" pouted John. Uncle Ruel's youngest sons were about the same age as John and I.

"Because they've already been exposed," Mother said. "I'll send 'em outside to play with y'all."

"What's 'exposed'?" I asked.

"They've already been where the bad germs are, may already have 'em in their bodies. Y'all haven't." *Oh.*

As for the malaria, no one knows how it came to coal country. A mosquito-borne disease, it is rare in Kentucky, even though mosquitoes are not. But, theorized the doctor who treated me, the mosquito that carried my illness probably migrated to coal country on the dragline transported from South America to the nearby strip mine. Or one of the South American workers who traveled to the States with the dragline might have been ill with malaria in the past. If he still carried in his body the malaria-causing parasite, a mosquito could have bitten him and transferred the parasite when it bit me. Regardless of how malaria invaded coal country, it invaded me with vengeance.

Two things I remember about the first of my three childhood encounters with the risks of life in coal country. One was Daddy carrying me outside to the quilt Mother had laid on the ground underneath a tree in the front yard. "Let's get you out here where it's cooler," said Daddy. "Them bad ol' 'skeeters!"

I had never before lain on my back and looked straight up into the branches of a tree from underneath it, nor had I ever noticed the patches of blue peeking among the fluttering leaves. *Oh, look how tall the tree is. And the sky is so blue!* "We've got to cool her down," said Mother as she and Daddy dipped washcloths into a pan of ice water and bathed my feverish body.

The other thing I remember is the dreadful-tasting quinine Mother forced down my throat daily. Pharmaceutical manufacturers would eventually provide powdered quinine in gelatin capsules that isolate the patient from the evil taste of the remedy, but the quinine prescribed for me was in liquid form.

For all my squirming and kicking, I was no match for Mother, who apparently knew nothing about a spoonful of sugar making the medicine go down. When I clamped my teeth together as a defense against the quinine, she simply pinned me to her side with one arm, pinched my nostrils shut and waited. When I involuntarily gasped for air—*glug!*—down went the healing quinine, spooned in by Dr. Mom. *Yuk! I'd rather have malaria than swallow this awful stuff!* Such foolishness was born of feverish delirium that left me with no memory of the illness itself, only the cure.

The ordeal of the quinine never got easier, except for Mother, who benefited greatly when I finally stopped protesting and surrendered to my fate. And according to doctor's orders, my torment at the hands of the vile-tasting liquid dragged on throughout the summer and repeated itself during the next two summers, a precaution against malaria's potential return even after the chills and fever were gone.

We had fought separate battles with foreign invaders, Uncle Ruel and I. Win one, lose one.

One-Room Schoolhouse

"You watch out for your little sister, now," Mother told John that day as she turned to leave us with the teacher and the other students. *I wish she'd quit sayin' that. John always gets to be my boss. I'm the littlest and I never get to be his boss!*

I had turned six and could say my ABCs, and it was finally my turn to go to school. Another Miss Mary was the teacher this year, and she didn't board with us. She wore her dark hair pulled back in a twist at the nape of her neck, and a decided overbite that kept her from completely closing her lips also kept her from being as pretty as the first Miss Mary. But this Miss Mary was nice, and her brown eyes crinkled at the corners when she smiled.

Yes, Miss Mary said when Mother handed her the bottle of quinine, she would give me a spoonful every day at noon until mosquito season was over. The only adult in a roomful of children, she was now not just a teacher, but also a nurse.

The white frame one-room schoolhouse held the teacher's desk and chair, a corner table holding a glass water jug with a metal spout, a black potbellied stove, and several rows of student desks of gradually increasing sizes screwed into the bare oiled floor. In the desks was storage space for books, supplies and the bag lunches that students brought from home, together with an aluminum cup to take to the water jug when we were thirsty. On the wall behind the teacher's desk was a room-spanning blackboard topped with the alphabet in both capital and lower case cursive letters. Centered above the alphabet, George Washington looked down on us from a gold-framed picture.

Another girl and a boy sat in the first grade row with me. John sat across the aisle from us in the row of three second-graders, the third-graders in the row beyond, and on up through the eighth grade, where the two Carriway boys sat. Held back two or three years for unsatisfactory performance, Harry and Henry clearly resented being there.

"Mr. and Miz Carriway don't care anything about education," Mother grumbled when we saw them walking down the sidewalk in Madisonville one Saturday afternoon. "No wonder their boys don't study."

Bigger than the other kids in school, the brothers were about the same size—at least two inches taller than Miss Mary and many pounds heavier. Their voices sounded like grown men's voices and their stringy dark blonde hair fell low across their brows, almost obscuring their menacing eyes. They shoved their hands into their pockets and hunched their shoulders forward when they walked, as though daring anyone to approach them. Their posturing worked; I was afraid of them.

When it was time for our lesson, Miss Mary called the first-graders up to the backless bench in front of her desk. When she finished our lesson, she sent us back to our desks and called the second-graders to come to the bench. After them, she called the third-graders, gradually working her way up until kids from all eight grades had taken their turn up front on the teaching bench. But if I behaved myself and didn't talk without first raising my hand and receiving permission, I could sit on the bench with the other classes and listen to their lessons. I often did that. Miss Mary varied the routine only in winter, when she moved the teaching bench closer to the potbellied stove with its open pan of water on top, evaporation humidifying the dry winter air.

One day when Miss Mary turned her back to write on the blackboard, Harry Carriway stood up at his desk, snapped open the blade of a long pocketknife and threw it at Miss Mary's back. Boing! The knife hit the blackboard and stuck there, waving back and forth beside Miss Mary's right arm.

Oh, my goodness! Horrified, I waited expectantly. After what seemed an eternity, Miss Mary slowly turned around, her voice belying the quietness of her movement. "Out! Of! My! Room!" she shouted, an index finger sharply punching the air after each word, eyes locked with those of the still-standing boy. "And don't *ever* come back!"

For one long moment, the defiant teenager hesitated, as though considering his options. Then, scowling as if he were the offended party, he stalked wordlessly out the door, his brother one step behind him.

In the uneasy silence that followed, the attention of 25 shocked kids squarely on Miss Mary's face, she turned her back to us and yanked the knife out of the blackboard. "School dismissed," she said quietly, knife in hand and face averted.

Darting unsure glances at one another, we hastily gathered our belongings and left in uncharacteristic quietness, too stunned to be excited that we were getting out of school early. Just as I reached the door, I looked back over my shoulder at Miss Mary. She was still at the blackboard, face in hands and shoulders shaking.

I'm not sure whether I heard her sobs or only imagine them in retrospect, but this I know: she had passed a test. To keep control of the youngest student, she had to gain control of the oldest.

I would live to rue the day she passed her test.

Mother Load

Lucy inserted between my lips the tip of a four-inch long piece of dried grapevine, the ash on the other end glowing. Then the sixth grade girl instructed me. "Just hold your nose and suck in, really hard, and the smoke will come into your mouth."

We were inside the girls' outhouse at school, five or six other older girls standing outside to keep watch. "If you won't tell on us for smokin'," Lucy had said, "we'll give you a puff."

"I won't tell," I promised, falling for the trick. Of course I wouldn't tell—not after I had participated!

Neither Mother nor Daddy smoked. Mother thought no one should smoke, and Daddy had seen so much tuberculosis that he refused to put anything in his lungs except air. Or perhaps more than tuberculosis, he feared black lung disease. He could not know that decades later he would pass from this world to the next miraculously free of the disease that plagued many underground coal miners after a lifetime of breathing coal dust. Whatever the reason, neither Daddy nor anyone in his family smoked. But Mother's father and brothers smoked, and in a state known for its burly tobacco farms, smoking was very common. Still, the grownups I'd seen smoking didn't seem to work at it as hard as I was working. I couldn't seem to draw the smoke through the porous vine into my mouth, no matter how hard I tried.

Suddenly, the door of the outhouse swung open and there stood Miss Mary. "You know it's against the rules to smoke on the school grounds!" she spat out, hands on hips and eyes blazing.

I didn't, although if I had thought, I would have known something was wrong with what we were doing. Otherwise, I wouldn't have had to promise not to tell, and we wouldn't have been hiding. Still, I was surprised when Miss Mary marched us inside, lined us up in front of the other students and began to spank us, one by one. Starting with Lucy, Miss Mary worked her way down to me.

The wait was agonizing. But wait I did, while each punished girl yelped and hopped around in a futile effort to avoid Miss Mary's thrashing hand, afterward slinking miserably to a seat. *Maybe Miss Mary'll be tired by the time she gets to me.* But she wasn't—at least, not as far as I could tell.

When it was over, it wasn't over—for the last of the hardened criminals to reap the consequences of our actions that day still had to go home when school was out. And even worse than the whipping was the fear of what Mother would do when I got there. She was the disciplinarian, so Daddy was not a worry—just Mother. *John thinks he's my boss and he's gonna tell on me. Blabbermouth!*

I knew it was no good asking him not to tell. Mother expected him to keep her informed, and if he didn't, he would be in trouble, too, when she found out. And with the obligatory eyes in the back of her head and the proverbial ear to the ground, she would find out. She *always* found out.

Sure enough, when we went home that afternoon, John told Mother.

Now, when Mother was furious, she was loquacious, her pent-up energy spewing forth in a cascade of words. "My kids don't misbehave in school!" she fumed, pacing up and down across the

67

kitchen floor. "What do you mean, Carole Sue, lettin' other people lead you around by the nose? You don't have to do somethin' just because somebody else tells you to! You've got a head. Use it! I never in my life—"

I'd rather take a whippin' than get Mother mad at me.

The next day, Mother went to school to talk to Miss Mary. Corporal punishment was acceptable in schools, so the spanking wasn't the issue. The issue was what Mother needed to do to help Miss Mary keep me under control.

Miss Mary felt bad about spanking me, she said, because she knew the older girls had led me astray. But she had to spank them, and she couldn't spank them without spanking me, too. Anyway, that's what Mother reported to Daddy that night, being sure that I was there to hear the full report. "I guess you'd better start behavin' yourself, little girl," said Daddy mildly.

"But I *am* bein' hav," I insisted.

They collapsed into laughter, my naive word twist saving me from more scolding. But every morning for days afterward, Mother repeated the same mantra when John and I left for school. "No more breakin' rules, little girl, or the next time, you're gonna be in *real* trouble." *Gonna be? If this is not real trouble, what is?*

The question weighed heavily on my mind. It was a Mother load.

Evening the Odds

After the Carriways, the next meanest kids were Billy and Bobby Joe York. They were smaller than the Carriways, but both Yorks were bigger than John, and Billy was older. His slicked-down black hair, olive skin and lanky body contrasted with Bobby's red hair, freckles and stocky build as much as Bobby's rowdy peskiness contrasted with Billy's brooding surliness.

For all of their differences, the brothers had at least one thing in common. They picked on John at school, sometimes following us home, throwing rocks at John's feet, taunting him and threatening him with sticks. The concept of fair play was apparently foreign to them; two on one was simply good odds. And they evidently considered me unworthy of their belligerence, for they never included me in their taunts.

One day, Billy's threats moved to action and he punched John. Standing by with fists poised, Bobby Joe was fully prepared to come to his older brother's aid if necessary. It wasn't.

"Well, what did you do when he hit you, John?" asked Mother when he went home crying.

"Nothin'," he said, eyes downcast.

"Nothin'?" Mother was aghast. "Nothin'? Son, nothin's not good enough," she shrieked. "You can't just let them beat you up. You've gotta defend yourself! If they know you won't take up for yourself, they'll just keep pickin' on you." Sandwiched between two older and two younger brothers, Mother almost certainly was drawing on her personal experience with childhood conflict.

The next day, Billy and Bobby Joe jumped John again. This time when we told Mother, she was even angrier than the first time. "John Morgan," she said, her voice tightly controlled. *Uh-oh, she's usin' her serious voice, not her angry voice. She's not just poppin' off this time.* "If you don't defend yourself the next time they jump on you, I'm gonna—" Then she turned to me. "And Carole Sue, the next time they jump on John, don't just stand there. You *help* him!"

"But I thought we weren't supposed to fight." It was more of a question than a statement.

"You're not. You won't *be* fightin'. You'll be defendin!" *Oh.*

By the time I noticed the fight the next day at recess, the two bullies had John down on the ground, arms and legs flailing, dust flying and all three of them rolling around in the dirt screaming at one another.

Mother's words ringing in my ears, I hesitated not one second. Picking up a downed tree limb, I walked up behind a completely oblivious Billy and Bobby Joe, who by now had John on his back desperately struggling to push them off. Raising the limb over my head with both hands, I swiftly brought the weapon down across the backs of the two unsuspecting bullies—whack! I had pulled back for another blow when they jumped up and started backing off. "I'm gonna tell Miss Mary on you," screamed Bobby Joe, his angry face nearly as red as his hair.

"You'll be sorry, you just wait and see!" shouted Billy, shaking his fist at me. Then he and Bobby Joe turned and ran.

"All right," said Miss Mary when the bell summoned us back inside and Bobby Joe told her what had happened—except for the part about the attack on John. "I want to see it. You go outside and bring me the limb she hit you with."

My heart jumped up into my throat. *Oh, no, she's gonna whip me again!* Another whipping at the hands of my teacher was sure to meet Mother's definition of real trouble.

Bobby Joe returned, dragging a much bigger limb than I had used, one obviously too heavy for me to lift. If I could see the lie, Miss Mary could see it, too. But that type of thinking was more sophisticated than I was, and I was too scared to speak, almost too scared to think. *He's lyin', Miss Mary, he's lyin'.*

Miss Mary didn't even look in my direction. "Bobby Joe, I'm ashamed of you," she said, eyes narrowed to threatening slits. "You take that limb back outside where you found it. And don't you dare ever lie to me again!" Bobby Joe turned in the direction of Miss Mary's pointing finger, backing off for the second time that day. *Dumb ol' Bobby Joe. He can't even lie his way out of trouble!*

Had Bobby Joe not stretched the truth the day I evened John's odds, I have no idea what would have been the outcome. But it was of no consequence to Daddy, who told and retold the story to friends and family for years afterward. "Don't mess with them Harris women," he bragged, laughing.

"Them Sisk women, you mean," Mother joked, putting her lineage in friendly competition with Daddy's.

I didn't care which side of the family got the credit, as long as I got my share. And I always did.

One Step Ahead

We were almost hypnotized, John and I, by the smooth, rhythmic flow of the huge dark green dragline working behind Mr. Parham's barn. The gigantic machine had rolled in on its caterpillar treads and was now working in the monstrous hole the miners had dynamited in the ground. Excavation its main job, the dragline routinely stripped away the layers of rock and soil covering the seam of coal so close to the earth's surface as to render more expensive underground mining unnecessary.

With its giant metal scoop suspended on a steel wire cable from a crane, the machine cast the bucket to the ground and dug its saw-toothed edge deeply into the earth. Scraping and digging its way along, the scoop gobbled up great mouthfuls of dirt and surface debris as it ponderously crawled toward the machine, pulled across the ground by another cable: the dragline. Once the scoop was full, the machine elevated its load high above the ground and rotated on its swivel base until the burden hung directly over the top of the spoil bank beside the excavation site. Only then did the scoop open its mammoth jaws and spill its capture onto the rising mound now growing taller with each bucketful of discarded earth.

"Fire in the hole," shouted a miner. I looked up to see Mother sprinting across the yard toward John and me. *Why is Mother runnin'?* She reached us a split second before I heard the blast and

71

felt the almost simultaneous rumble, then the spray of dirt and bits of rock that showered down upon us. I had heard the warning but had understood neither its meaning nor exactly what had just happened. Nor did I realize that I had just survived my second encounter with the risks of life in coal country.

"You kids come in the house right this minute," Mother cried, grabbing us each by the hand. *Mother says 'right this minute' a lot.* Hurrying us onto the back porch, she brushed the debris out of our hair and off our clothes. The only hurt was Mother's fright.

Once she had us inside the house, she squatted down to our eye level. "The next time you hear a man yell out, 'Fire in the hole,' that means they're gonna set off dynamite," she said, urgency in her voice. "Don't wait till you hear the blast; just run as fast as you can to the house. Don't stop to pick up your toys or anything." *Don't pick up our toys? I've never heard of a good reason for not pickin' up our toys.*

That night, Mother told Daddy about the dynamite. "The strip mine's gettin' too close for comfort," she concluded. "It's not safe for the kids."

We moved before school was out. Our walk to school was longer now, following a worn footpath through the woods and approaching the school from a different direction. At the end of the year, Mother took our report cards and locked them in the cedar chest with John's first grade report card. *Our report cards are in the cedar chest? I didn't know they were that important!*

"The strip mine's progressin' and they're gonna tear down Wilson schoolhouse," Mother told us. "Next year, they're gonna send a school bus to take you kids to the big consolidated school at Anton."

We had been chased out of our home one step ahead of a strip mine, and now we were being chased out of our school one step ahead of a demolition crew. It wasn't remarkable; it was just coal country.

I suppose it was a good thing. At least we were ahead.

A Very Big But

The mine owned the house we lived in, one of three small white frame houses with dingy, fading paint sited in a short line of houses informally known as Bosses Row. It was a misnomer. If they ever had been, the houses were no longer restricted to bosses and their families.

To get to Bosses Row from the Parham house, we turned north, went past Wilson school, crossed the railroad tracks, turned west onto the access road running alongside the railroad tracks to Pine Hill coal mine, and went past the mine about a quarter of a mile to the house. It was the first time we had lived close enough to other people to see their houses from ours.

In the house next to us lived the Harpers. Their oldest son was almost grown, too old to play with John and me. But the other Harper kids—Joyce, Marilyn and Jerry—soon became our friends. The girls were older than John and me, and Jerry was my age.

On the other side of the Harpers lived the Yorks with Billy and Bobby Joe, the bullies John and I already knew were not our friends.

Our house was on the end of the row nearest the 10-foot-wide ditch running inside the fence that enclosed the lane the 15 to 20 mules walked down every morning on their way from the Strongs' farm to the mine for a day's work. "You stay on this side of the fence," Mother told John and me. "Don't ever get in the water. It's over your heads. Daddy has to teach you how to swim before you get in the water!"

Aw, Mu-thur! "But how can we learn to swim without gettin' in the water?"

"Don't smart off to me, young lady, or—" *Okay, okay.*

Once the mules were at the mine, a miner led them, two at a time, onto the cage, where they rode to the bottom of the shaft and began their work pulling mini-railcars along steel tracks to and from the

73

cage. Each day after work, the mules rode back up on the cage and funneled into a chute that channeled them into the lane, where they trudged back to the Strongs' farm for food and rest.

The yard in front of our house was in no respect a lawn. Merely bare earth underneath the shade of a few maple trees and an oak that teased the squirrels with the acorns it dropped on the ground, the hard-packed soil was completely devoid of grass. In the summer and fall, Mother broom-swept the yard to rid it of dropped leaves, twigs and other debris.

But the yard had one major asset: a sweet gum tree, like the one of gum ball fame at the Wagner place. I was surprised to learn that the sweet gum concealed a syrupy substance worthy of its name. Taking a tip from Mother, John and I lanced a two-inch cut in the trunk. Within a couple of weeks, we chipped away the drippings that oozed out as a liquid and dried as an amber resin on the furrowed bark. The gum wasn't as tasty as commercially produced chewing gum, and the resin stuck to our teeth if we put it in our mouths while it was still tacky to our fingers. But if we waited until the gum was dry, it provided a good substitute for the commercial variety until we could get to Miz Bessie's store with our nickel.

The only variation our house boasted from the standard four-rooms-and-a-path was a small breakfast nook off the kitchen formed by closing in one end of the back porch. But—and this is a very big "but"—from the center of the ceiling in each room hung a cord that sprouted a bare light bulb!

Rural electrification had not yet made its way to that area of Kentucky, but the mine owner had stretched electrical wiring to the house from the generator at the mine. No more storing kerosene in a can on the back porch, no more filling kerosene lamps, no more trimming blackened wicks, no more washing and polishing smoky glass chimneys, no more carrying lamps from room to room at night, no more squinting eyes to read after dark.

The house at the mine was smaller and shabbier than the Parham house with its massive mantelpieces, big rooms and center entrance hall. But now we had light, wondrous light—and all for the flip of a switch.

It was a switch well worth the move.

Modern Conveniences

"Quick, Sterlin'," urged Mother, "it's gettin' ready to blow up a storm." Dropping *The Madisonville Messenger* beside the chair where he was reading, Daddy raced outside to move the rain barrel from underneath the eaves of the house.

This was a process new to me, but now that we lived near the mine, coal dust settled heavily on the roof of our house, and the first catch of rainwater was too dirty to use for laundry. Mother and Daddy solved this problem by moving the barrel so it didn't catch the first rain that fell, waiting until the rain had washed the roof, then running outside in the rain and moving the barrel back underneath the eaves. It required a watchful eye on the skies and a willingness to get wet, but it was a small price to pay for clean, soft laundry water.

Washday wasn't as bad it used to be, thanks to the new electric wringer washing machine. Of course, Mother still had to carry the water in buckets from the barrel outside, and still had to fire up the kitchen range to heat the water, and still had to wash Daddy's work clothes in a lye-water kettle outside. But washday was much less stressful now than before we moved to the mine, and Mother's disposition showed it.

I was old enough to help with the laundry when I wasn't in school, and I loved helping. It was fun pulling the clothes out of the sudsy water and slowly feeding them, one piece at a time, between the wringer's two rotating rubber rollers. After the clothes fell into the waiting tub of rinse water on the other side of the wringer, I shifted the wringer a half-round until it hung over the rinse tub, and repeated the wringing process for a second rinse in another tub. Putting the clothes through the wringer for a final time, I allowed the clothes to fall into a basket, which Mother and I carried to the clothesline.

Not tall enough to reach the line, I handed the clothespins and wet clothes to Mother, one piece at a time, for pinning up to dry. "I hope I never have to even *look* at another washboard," she smiled. "I mean never!" *If you hope you don't, what do you think I hope?*

Other electrical conveniences eventually came: a refrigerator, an iron, a radio and a few lamps. The wiring in the house wasn't powerful enough to operate an electric range, and although the new range wasn't electric, it was an improvement over the previous one. Above the cooking surface of the new range was a warming oven, and below it on one side was a reservoir into which Mother poured water for heating by the fire in the adjacent but separate chamber. Warm water to wash our faces in the morning—what a luxury!

We had no telephone, but it was not an inconvenience. We didn't know anyone who had a phone, so why would we need one?

But a coal-burning Warm Morning heater? That was different. We eventually transitioned to one from open fireplaces, and it was not just a more efficient use of coal, it was a more effective way to heat the house. The stove sat out beyond the hearth on a metal fire-retardant pad, the fireplace covered with a metal shield and the stovepipe vented through the shield to the chimney. The stove demanded a lot more space in the room than did the fireplace, and the Warm Morning wasn't nearly as attractive as the fireplace, but Mother and Daddy had made a pragmatic swap: beauty for warmth.

We were making progress in steps. At first, we were a step ahead. Now we were a step up.

Quitting Time

Standing on our decrepit front porch, John and I looked at the tipple, then looked at each other, then looked back at the tipple. Fascinated with the tipple's workings when we first moved to the mine, we were now bored with the repetition, tired of the monotony.

The cage, carrying a mini-railcar, rode its steel wire cable up the vertical shaft to the top of the tipple straddling a spur off the main railroad track, tilted the car and dumped a load of coal onto the shaker. As the cage slid back down the cable for more coal, the huge metal shaker shuddered in rickety-rackety vibration, sifting the coal through holes of different dimensions that sorted and graded the chunks by size to be transported out in the railcars waiting below. And it repeated the process time after time, day after day, sometimes even on Saturday and Sunday.

Finally, the late afternoon steam whistle blew—whoo! whoo! whoo!—the three blasts announcing quitting time. "That's it," said John. *I know, I know.* The next time the cage climbed up the shaft, it would carry a load of men instead of coal, and it would stop at ground level instead of sliding on up the tipple.

From our vantage point on the front porch, the miners exiting the cage were indistinguishable one from the other, all as black as soot no matter what color they were when they went underground that morning. They all wore clompy protective steel-toed shoes, a headlamp clipped above the bill of their hard caps. Attached to an electric power cord that snaked down the miners' backs to a portable battery swinging from their belts, the headlamp beamed the indispensable light that provided visibility underground.

Daddy was easy to spot getting off the cage, his cap the only bright red one in an ocean of bobbing black caps. But I could have spotted Daddy, even without his red hard cap. "It's that Harris walk,"

Mother said. "They all walk like that, sort of like they swing one hip more than the other."

Sometimes John and I ran down the lane to meet Daddy when he headed home, hoping that he had stashed a surprise for us in his pocket, something found that day in the mine. A pretty colored stone or an oddly shaped one. A fossilized fern formed millions of years earlier during The Coal Age. A geode, a hollow orb-shaped stone lined with sparkling clear crystals inside. A piece of pyrite, known informally as fool's gold: a hard and shiny yellow mineral generally found in the form of cube-shaped opaque crystals and nicknamed for its visual similarity to unprocessed gold.

Once, Daddy's find was too big for him to carry in his pocket, so he carried it in his hands: a heavy black stone formed in the shape of a person with only one leg. We dubbed the find One-Legged Pete, and he earned his keep for years by serving as a doorstop.

Occasionally, the surprise would be something not from inside the mine at all, but a small token gift brought to Daddy by one of his crew. From a miner proud to be the father of a new baby girl, a piece of pink bubblegum shaped and wrapped to look like a cigar. From a miner who didn't know that Daddy was a teetotaler, a miniature bottle of Kentucky bourbon, its red seal still intact. From a miner who had recently returned from a trip to the Grand Ole Opry, a picture postcard bearing a full color map of the state of Tennessee. Except for One-Legged Pete, Mother took all of our treasures and locked them in the cedar chest. "I'll keep your things safe for you," she said.

We had learned not to reach for Daddy's hand when we went to meet him. "I'm too dirty," he had said the first time. "Wait till I get my bath." So we walked by his side, taking turns carrying his lunch bucket and wondering if he had eaten all the fig bars Mother had packed for his lunch that day. If he hadn't, he would give them to us.

Daddy had to keep reminding us not to take his hand, though, because we kept forgetting about the coal dust. Oh, we could see it all right, we just didn't care. For to us, Daddy wasn't dirty. He was Daddy.

Never Say Goodbye

"'Bye, Daddy." It was our duet, John's and mine. We sang it every morning when Daddy cupped Mother's chin in his hand and gave her a big sloppy-mouthed kiss before he left for the mine. It happened every time he went to work, no matter what. I had seen them stop in the full throes of an argument for the kiss, only to pick up the dispute again as soon as Daddy walked back into the house.

"I thought you and Daddy were mad at each other," I said to Mother after the kiss, puzzled about what I thought was strange behavior.

"But we don't stay mad. You know what the Bible says: 'Get rid of your anger before the sun goes down.'" *Well, the way you and Daddy act, you'd think it said, 'Don't let a man go down into the coal mine without a kiss from his wife.'*

"But—"

"Honey, your daddy's a coal miner," she interrupted, as though that it explained it. It did. But not to a six-year-old.

Now almost out the door, Daddy gave a half turn. "Be good babies," he smiled, throwing us a wave as he closed the door behind him. *How come he's like that? He never says 'bye.*

"Mother, why doesn't Daddy ever say 'bye back to us?" Of all the times I had noticed it, even been frustrated by it, I had never thought to ask the question.

"Honey, your daddy's a coal miner." *There it is again, the same answer to a different question.*

"I know. But why doesn't he ever say 'bye back to us?"

"He never will. I've never heard him say it. Not to you, not to me, and not to anybody else, either. If he says 'bye, it's kinda like he really means it. I mean, it's like he thinks he'd be invitin' disaster and it would be a *real* goodbye and he'd never come back home again."

"But Daddy always comes back home," I argued. For if anything in our family was predictable, it was that Daddy would go to the mine in the morning and come back home in late afternoon.

"I know, but—" Mother turned away, clearly through with the discussion. *I guess there are some things you've just gotta be grown to understand.*

Spared by her obliqueness, I knew nothing of the hazards of Daddy's occupation, nothing of the risk he willingly assumed in the support of our family. And nothing about the fear that he looked squarely in the eye and stared down when he stepped onto the cage every morning.

It would be years before an increased emphasis on mining safety would greatly reduce the number of fatalities in America's coal mines, and years before Mother's words would replay themselves in my mind.

And when they did, they wrapped their gnarly fingers around my heart and squeezed out the tears.

Stirring Up Rainbows

"Don't pull up those ol' weeds!" ordered John, tossing me a backward glance. "They'll make you sneeze." *He thinks he's my boss just because he's in the second grade and I'm only in the first. But that doesn't make him my boss. I don't have to mind him, and I'm not goin' to!*

We gradually worked our way down the road toward the bank of mailboxes for Bosses Row. While John entertained himself by sailing flat rocks at the ground to kick up dust, I dawdled along behind taking care of important business: plucking goldenrods from the side of the road to make a bouquet.

"They're not weeds!" I argued, defending the maligned plants that he and others considered a nuisance but I considered wildflowers, beautiful even if their fragrance wasn't. I fully intended to surprise Mother with a handful of them in a green-tinted Ball jar filled with water, regardless of what John said. I had visions of our family at supper that night, the flowers gracing our oilcloth-covered kitchen table and brightening our otherwise drab surroundings. "And they don't make me sneeze, either," I disputed, continuing my defense of the goldenrods.

On the other side of the road was a shallow stream that carried storm water runoff from the mine's outside operations, where countless bits of coal and rock flaked off the processed coal and lay on the ground like breadcrumbs on a kitchen floor. Scraped up and piled into huge slack heaps, these worthless fragments yielded to the inevitable rains that raced across their shiny black surfaces and leached out the minerals, flushing them into the stream. The resultant copper-colored groundwater had the appearance of redeye gravy, and it was just as greasy, though it tasted not at all like the delicious pan drippings left in the skillet where Mother had fried country ham.

I knew this, because I had once confirmed it by dipping into the water an index finger and touching it to the tip of my tongue. One taste was enough. The sample had a distinctly metallic tang much like the copper penny I had once held in my mouth for a few seconds before Mother caught me and insisted that I spit it out.

I didn't intend to taste the coppery water again; still, it captured my attention. Squatting on the bank of the stream, I laid my goldenrods down and lightly trailed a finger in the water, gently swirling the patch of oil floating on the surface and watching the glinting sunlight flash tiny shimmers across the iridescent colors.

"Quit playin' in that awful stuff," growled John, frowning at coal country's industrial pollution. "It's dirty!"

"I'm not playin'," I protested. "I'm strirrin' up rainbows."

The puzzled look on John's face told me he didn't understand. I didn't care and I didn't explain. *How can he be my boss? He doesn't even know as much as I know.* Undeterred from my goal, I picked up my treasured goldenrods and moved on. And that night, just as I envisioned, my disparaged bouquet found a place of honor on our family supper table.

We can see heaven in a wildflower, wrote poet William Blake two centuries earlier. And then he cautioned: never doubt what you see, for if you do, you'll never believe.

I have never doubted what I saw that day, and today I believe in the transcendent power of beauty. For I have seen William Blake's heaven in a wildflower. And I have seen my very own rainbows in coal country.

Four. Rainbow Mercy

Rainbow arch, thy mercy's sign . . .[4]
— Oliver Wendell Holmes

Leading the Way

When we walked to the school bus stop, where we joined six or seven other kids from the mining camp just north of the stop, John led the way straight down the road beside the railroad track. It was right that he should lead; he was starting third grade and I was starting second.

Usually, because all the kids from Bosses Row were on the same schedule, we walked with Joyce, Marilyn and Jerry Harper, and the two York brothers. Not surprisingly, we talked very little to Billy and Bobby Joe. In the cold aftermath of thwarted aggression, our opposing camps had developed an unspoken agreement: if they didn't bother us, we wouldn't bother them.

Soon we learned the pattern. A train always passed, towing away the coal from the previous day's work at the mine. We jumped up and down, waving to the engineer and shouting, "Hey, Mr. Engineer—hey!" We knew he couldn't hear us above the roar of the train and the rattle of wheel against rail, but we hoped he'd see us jumping and flailing our arms in the air. He learned to watch for us, for he usually leaned out the window and waved just before sounding the whistle to signal his approach to the upcoming railroad crossing.

On rainy afternoons as we walked home, John led us across to the railroad tracks so we could avoid the muddy road by walking on the wooden ties between the steel rails. Occasionally, we dared to step up onto one of the rails, arms held out to our sides at shoulder height to balance ourselves.

It was a risk we willingly took in full knowledge that when we slipped, we almost certainly would bruise the ankle that slid down the side of the rail before coming to an abrupt halt on the rocks or tie below. Mother and Daddy had walked on the railroad tracks as children, they said, and we knew sight and sound would give us plenty of warning to escape the danger of an unlikely approaching train, either ahead of us or in back.

In winter when snow turned the ground white, John made tracks for me to step in. "My feet are bigger than yours," he would say. "Step where I step." I did, happy to keep my bootless feet dry.

It was a forecast of the future, John making a path for me to follow. "Oh, so you're John's sister," my teachers always said at the beginning of the school year. "John did a good job last year. But you're a good student, too, I hear." And because inspiration comes from those who set the standard, I never considered not meeting it.

It didn't matter that John couldn't see elephants in the sky or rainbows in groundwater. He set the standard high and he led the way.

First Love

The school bus was cavernous, especially since ours was the first stop in the morning and the bus was empty when the kids from Bosses Row boarded. But as the driver made more stops for more students, the bus seemed to shrink until it was barely big enough to accommodate everyone standing in the aisle. By now, high school had come to coal country, even though the school had yet to meet accreditation standards. Each of the 12 grades had a separate room in Anton's building, and many of the students in the higher grades were as big as grown men and women. *More kids are on this bus than were in my whole school last year. Anton must be a big school!*

I soon chose my favorite seat: the side bench up front across from

Chuck, the driver. For before my dangling legs could reach the floor, before I knew what a crush was, one had me by the heart. *He's so handsome, and he always smiles at me. He smiles at me even more than he smiles at anyone else.* I reveled in my front seat.

One day, Chuck abruptly jammed on the brakes to avoid a stopping car. Sailing out of the slick seat, I skidded onto the floor in a scrambling fall that landed me rump-first at the bottom of the step well for the door. Every kid on the bus, captive witness to my startled embarrassment, turned toward the sound, necks craning and eyes searching to see what had happened. "Are you all right?" asked Chuck, his brown eyes fixed on my crimson face.

Stifling the tears that fought mightily for release, I channeled my humiliation into anger and mustered all the aplomb a second-grader could muster. Stomping up the steps, I looked him straight in the eye. "Don't you *ever* do that to me again!" I yelled, eyeing him fiercely as I crawled back up into my seat.

"I'm sorry," he said, an amused smile playing across his lips as the bus began to move again. *He's laughin' at me! He's laughin' at me and he thinks I don't know.*

Boarding the bus after school that afternoon, I haughtily passed Chuck by in favor of a seat in the back where he couldn't see me. I couldn't see him, either, and didn't want to.

It served him right. He wasn't good enough for me, anyway.

Independent Learning

To my assigned seat in the middle of the second grade room came a grinding sound. *What's that noise?* Shortly, out of the corner of one eye, I saw a classmate slide back into his seat and another classmate leave hers, pencil in hand, and walk quietly to the back of the room. Again came the grinding sound. Several times it happened that first day, the students taking full advantage of Miss Laura Raye's permission to move around the room whenever we wanted as long as we didn't disturb the other kids.

What are they doin'? What's makin' that grindin' sound? Heeding the clue of the pencil I had seen in the other students' hands, I grasped my pencil and eyed Miss Laura Raye. Now seated at her desk, she wore like a skull cap her tightly curled salt-and-pepper hair. Glasses on the tip of her nose, she occasionally looked up to keep an eye on us as she did whatever teachers do at their desks. I liked it when she was at her desk. I was leery of her when she walked around the room, toes pointed outward like a ballerina, creating no sound to alert us to her presence.

Very cautious about stern-faced Miss Laura Raye, I contemplated my action. Miss Mary had been all warm and smiley, but when I had made a mistake, she had whipped me. *No tellin' what Miss Laura Raye will do to me if I make a mistake. But she said it was okay to get up, so—*

Summoning all of my courage, I slid out of my seat and pretended casualness as I walked to the back of the room. *If I don't see somethin' I've never seen before, I'll go back to my seat and ask a question later.* But there it was, anchored to the windowsill: a small metal contraption with a crank handle on one side.

Carefully looking at but not touching the device, I spotted on the side opposite the crank a hole about as big around as my pencil. *I bet it's a thing that sharpens pencils.* Quickly, I concluded that I could turn the crank. Touching it tentatively, I gave it a slow whirl. *What if I do it wrong?* Furtively I looked around. *No one is watchin'. All right so far.* Heart beating wildly, I grasped my pencil and tightly pressed the writing tip into the hole. *If they can do it, I can do it, too.* Slowly I turned the crank, then faster. Sure enough, the familiar grinding sound started, gradually changing tone until it sounded smoother, a little less grating. *I'm gonna stop now and look at my pencil.*

To this child accustomed to her daddy sharpening her pencil with his pocketknife, it was an astonishing sight, purely and absolutely astonishing: the sharpest pencil point I had ever seen!

Silently I returned to my desk, unaware that I had put into practice two primary principles of learning: observation and experimentation. They would come to mark my approach to life, an approach that never let me down.

Nosing Around

"Wanna see a woman without a nose?" Betty Sue was living with Grandma and Grandpa Sisk now, and I was visiting.

"What?" I looked up from the paper dolls we were cutting out on Grandma's back porch. "Everybody's got a nose."

"Not her!" Betty was emphatic, a gleam in her brown eyes.

"Why not? Where did it go?"

"Doctor cut it off." Betty was smiling, aware that she had my complete attention. "Grandma said Miz Brown had a disease and the doctor cut her nose off."

I was curious, but I knew it was impolite to gawk at people with disabilities. Every time I saw someone with a missing arm or leg, or someone who rode in a wheelchair, Mother forbade me to stare, squeezing my hand tightly as she whispered the warning.

I thought about Betty's proposition. "Well, I guess I could just look, if I don't stare. It wouldn't hurt to just look, would it?"

"Nope. Never hurt me."

Oh, Betty Sue, for goodness sake! "I don't mean hurt you, silly; I mean hurt her."

Betty shrugged. "Naw, it won't hurt her. All we have to do is walk down to her house. We'll take her some cookies and she'll let us in and talk to us. I go to see her all the time. I'll tell her you're my cousin and I want her to meet you. She won't know we came just to look at her nose."

"I thought you said she didn't have a nose."

"She don't," said Betty crossly. "You know what I mean."

When we knocked on the door with Grandma's cookies, Miz Brown came and invited us in, took us into her kitchen, sat us down at her table and gave us each a glass of milk and one of the cookies we had brought. Sure enough, she had no nose, and she had covered the place where it had been with a white bandage. But she acted as if she didn't know, which made it easy for us to act the same way. *How does she breathe? Through her mouth, I guess. Like when you have a cold and your nose is all stuffed up.*

After a while, Miz Brown said thanks for the cookies and we said you're welcome and left. But after we got back to Grandma's, I was ashamed. It was wrong, pretending to be Miz Brown's friend so we could spy on her, even if we hadn't stared.

Of course, in all likelihood, she knew what we were doing and was kind enough to indulge our childish curiosity. She probably knew all along that we were just kids nosing around.

Got Milk?

"You kids take this jug up to Miz Strong's and see if she's got any milk. If she has, ask her to send me a gallon. Give her this," Mother said, handing John a dollar bill.

Miz Strong was a pretty woman—solid and stout, according to Miz Harper, who used the term as an euphemism for fat—large of size and heart with a white-toothed smile, dark shining eyes and beautiful gray-streaked wings in the temples of her wavy black hair. "I've got only boys," Miz Strong had said once, "but girls are real special." She had smiled at me when she said it. *I'm special—aha!*

John took the jug, stuffed the money into his pocket, and the two of us walked across the field to the farmhouse we could see in the distance. Besides boarding the mules for the mine, the Strongs were dairy farmers, and they sometimes had extra milk to sell to neighbors.

"Here's your mom's change," said Miz Strong, handing John the jug of milk and some coins. "Y'all come back to see me any time you want."

After we were home, Mother put the coins in her purse and the milk in the new refrigerator. The next morning, she poured our breakfast milk.

Suspecting nothing out of the ordinary, I lifted my glass and sipped. *Wow! What is this?* I held my glass at arm's length and studied it. *It looks like milk, but it tastes better 'n milk!* Big swallow this time. Umm—my lips, my mouth, my tongue! Laughing, frolicking, applauding with pleasure, my taste buds stood up on their hind legs and danced, right there inside my mouth! Who knew they could dance? Before this, they had been entirely passive, unquestioningly accepting of the nutritionally sound but boringly bland canned evaporated milk that John and I had learned to drink at room temperature in the absence of refrigeration.

"Like it, huh?" laughed Mother as John and I drained our glasses and licked the last drop off the rim. Then she stepped up to a challenge: convincing two dubious children that fresh milk and canned milk were the same beverage.

Life brings adjustments. And when it does, it's far easier to adjust to moving up than to moving down. People usually say that about money. I say it about milk.

Bedtime Prayer

"I double-dog dare you to keep your knees stiff this time," John taunted me. A dare is a dare, but a double-dog dare is a blatant affront.

"The kids are gettin' too old to sleep in the same bed," Mother had told Daddy weeks earlier. "We've gotta get twin beds for 'em."

I didn't know why; we hadn't complained. Oh, sometimes John protested when I lined up all my dolls and laid them on the pillow between us, but we worked things out. Mary Francis, Shirley Ann and Blue Rag Doll had joined Mary Jane by now, but after I agreed to put Blue Rag Doll next to John, he stopped complaining. Her head wasn't cold and hard if he happened to turn over on her during the night. Still, even the dolls were happy when John and I received our very own separate beds. I know, because Mary Jane told me so.

No self-respecting seven-year-old girl can let her eight-year-old brother get away with a double-dog dare! I climbed up on the headboard and leapt onto my new bed one more time, only this time, I didn't bend my knees. Quite a feat, if I do say so—next to impossible. And it *is* impossible to remain standing afterward, as I learned when I fell onto the floor.

Now, John and I both knew not to bounce up and down on the bed, but blasting ourselves feet first off the headboard onto the mattress was different. We both had already used our headboards as a launching pad to our mattresses at least three times that morning, except for the stiff knees part, and nothing bad had happened. But this time, with no give in my knees, something else had to give.

I knew it was bad news as soon as I heard the cracking sound followed by a muffled thud.

From my face-up position on the floor, I instinctively turned my head and looked under the bed. There, resting on the floor, were two splintered pointy ends of a broken slat, the bottom lining of the box springs ripped where the slat had punched through. And when I sat up and looked at the bed, I saw an even scarier thing: a wide swooping dip in the mattress. *Oh, no! Mother will absolutely kill me!* I knew this, because she had killed me many times before, and for less reason.

Only those who know the desperation of a child in trouble can know the desperation of a child's prayer. "Please, God, please fix the bed," I begged. "I was just playin'; I didn't know it would break the bed. Mother has never said, 'Don't get up on the headboard and jump off onto the bed,' she just said not to bounce on it." I earnestly told God all these things, and more, as I gazed at the framed picture of the Lord's Prayer hanging on the wall over my brand new broken bed.

Throughout the day, I periodically sneaked into the bedroom and looked to see if God had fixed the bed yet. No, not yet.

Maybe God's on vacation.

Oh, don't be silly. God doesn't go on vacation, He's on duty all the time.

I resorted to scheming. Mother had already made our beds that day, and she probably wouldn't go back into our bedroom until bedtime. If I worked it right, I could be all balled up in the bed and under the covers when she got there, and she wouldn't notice the damage. That would give God more time to fix the bed, if He needed more time. And clearly, even if He didn't need it, He intended to take it.

Sure enough, Mother didn't notice the broken bed that night, and John didn't tell on me—probably because he felt guilty about his part in the incident—so God had extra time to work His miracle. But by the next morning when the miracle hadn't happened, I knew I was in trouble.

A person given bad news remembers only a small percentage of anything said immediately afterward, the level of anxiety obscuring additional information. So today, I have no memory of what Mother said or did. All I remember is that I had to sleep in that sorry bed night after night forever, it seemed, until one day Grandpa Sisk came to our house with a strip of lumber and nailed a new slat onto the bottom of my bed.

God may not come when you call Him, but He always comes in time. Or sends someone else to help, like He sent Grandpa. I apparently sensed this, for I emerged from the experience completely unscathed, my childish faith wholly intact.

Perhaps that, itself, was the miracle.

No Place for a Girl

"I wanna go, I wanna go," I begged, jumping up and down. Daddy had started out the door toward the mine with John at his side.

"No," said Daddy firmly. "The mine's no place for a girl."

"Honey, it's just men over there," agreed Mother as Daddy closed the door behind him and John. "You stay here with me." Then she moved to make up for Daddy's typical paucity of words.

"Miners are funny about women," she said. "Legend has it that the worst mine disasters in the world happened right after a woman had been inside, so miners think women are bad luck. Your granddaddy used to take me inside with him to set the dynamite caps for the next day's work. But when I turned 12, the miners came to him and said, 'You've gotta leave the little gal out, now.' And he never took me back."

Daddy didn't take John underground, only up into the tipple and into the boiler room and some of the other outside buildings. And he never took John with him when the mine was running, only in late afternoon after quitting time or on a weekend when he went to do a safety check.

But one Saturday, for reasons still unknown to me, Daddy let me go to the mine with him and John. The boiler room was a low rumble of humming motors and a slow hiss of escaping steam, even though the mine wasn't working. And when Daddy turned one of the knobs to vent a valve on the boiler, the hissing steam mildly exploded—pa-skew!—startling me into wide-eyed fright even as I surveyed the room. The unpainted bare plank walls were gray and dingy, except for the brightly colored pictures of pretty and scantily clad women the men had used to decorate the room.

Noticing that I had spotted the pictures, Daddy hurried John and me up the stairs of the towering tipple. *Ooo, it's so high up here!* Everything about it was intimidating. Open wooden scaffolding. Rough creaky floor. Porous metal shaker. Puzzling mechanical devices. Thick steel cables. I clung to Daddy's hand, pretending I wasn't scared of all the strange sights and sounds.

Once back on ground, Daddy walked us to the train standing idly on a side track in preparation for towing away the full cars of coal from the prior day's work. Lifting me up, he set my feet on the bottom step leading into the engine cabin, then he lifted John up and stood him beside me. Reaching down and taking each of us by the hand, the engineer pulled us up the rest of the steps into the cabin, leaving Daddy standing on the ground at the door. *Ooo, it's so big in here!*

The engineer was dressed just like Overall Bill, his belly huge and the backs of his pudgy hands sprouting thick black hair. *Wonder if he's the one we see in the mornin' when we're walkin' to the school bus stop?* And the engine—what a maze of levers and numbered dials with red and black needles, and wheels and mysterious buttons, and metal switches and knobs to push and turn!

The next day at church, all the girls I told about my weekend tour listened with rapt attention and transparent envy, I the only one of us to have been inside a train engine, I the only one of us to have been inside a tipple.

None of us would have believed the changes the future would bring, nor would we have believed that laws ushering in the future would push superstition aside in favor of equal employment opportunity. But in the 1970s when it happened, women pioneers entered the mines in droves to claim the jobs that would feed their families, achieving equal pay with men and accepting equal risk, both underground and on the surface.

The coal mine is still no place for a girl. But now it is not just a place for men—it is also a place for women.

Weather Vain

It's cold this mornin', really cold. The night before, Mother had heated her irons on the kitchen range, wrapped them in strips torn from a worn flannel blanket and tucked a warm bundle into each of our beds. "Put your feet up against these," she told John and me. We needed no coaxing.

The room where John and I slept was the only room in the house with no fireplace, except for the kitchen, which drew heat from the range. On very cold days, we went into our bedroom only at bedtime. And perish the thought of getting up at night for the toilet! "Chamber pots, my eye," Mother said. "Forget those nasty things. Go on outside, like you're supposed to."

It was bad enough to have to go outside when it was cold, but it was even worse when it was cold and dark—a sharp contrast to using an indoor bathroom. I had experienced the latter more than once in the homes of three of Daddy's brothers who had done well enough to have houses in Madisonville where they lived with their families.

Uncle Clarence had parlayed one old fixer-up house into several rental properties, Uncle Vernon operated a saw mill, and Uncle Joe worked for the Madisonville City Water Department. When we visited them, I made it a point to "go" so I could flush the toilet and wash my hands with warm water for the mere twist of a knob. And I knew of a certainty: the best part about living in town was having an indoor bathroom when it was cold outside.

I had quickly escaped the bedroom for the warm kitchen that morning, and after breakfast, I began to dread the cold walk to the school bus. When I was younger, snowsuits had covered my legs in winter. But second-graders were too big for snowsuits, and long pants for girls and women were acceptable only for outdoor work and play. "You'll be all right," Mother said. "Pride has no pain." *What does she mean by that?* All I knew was that I wouldn't be wearing long pants to school.

But it was the very coldest of days, and Mother took pity on me. "Put these on," she said, pulling a pair of John's corduroy pants up underneath my skirt, buttoning them around my waist and pulling my skirt down over the pants. "Not the prettiest thing I've ever seen, but—" *Who cares?* "When you get to school, take the pants off and stuff 'em in your desk until it's time to get on the bus to come home."

"Why can't I just keep 'em on?" The schoolroom would be cold, too—not as cold as it was outside, but still cold.

"Girls don't wear pants in school." *Okay, okay.*

The summer was uncomfortable, too. With not a single electric fan in the house, we searched in vain for the slightest cooling breeze. One thing about the mine was good, Daddy said. It was always cool underground, a consistent temperature in the 60s.

The thing about the mine that wasn't good was the coal dust. My pale blond hair showed even the smallest black speck that fell on it, and since I played outside all summer long, the coal dust was the bane of my summer existence. "A little vanity does a woman a lotta good," said Mother, bending me over the wash basin and shampooing my hair every day, whether I liked it or not. Not!

Pride has no pain. A little vanity does a woman a lotta good. Two of Mother's favorite expressions, I dreaded them as signs of upcoming misery. And they were, every time.

First Dance

Daddy didn't dance and Mother didn't rock 'n' roll. But then, it wasn't their era.

"Swing your partner, do-si-do!" rang out the voice of the caller, the line of square dancers a pulsing labyrinth of twisting, turning movement. Daddy, fiddle underneath his chin and bow arm in constant motion, stood on the school gymnasium's stage with a couple of guitarists and a bass fiddler. THUMP, thump, THUMP, thump went the steady bass beat as Daddy's melody soared above the picking and strumming of the guitar.

I sat beside Mother on the bleachers. "Your daddy and your Uncle Joe used to play for all the square dances," Mother said. "I never did get to dance with your daddy because he was always playin' fiddle. But he didn't mind if I danced with Ben Sellers, as long as I didn't leave the room with him."

"Really?"

"Uh-huh. And poor ol' Ben! He liked me before your daddy came along. The roads were so bad then that we used to wear our old shoes when we went somewhere. We'd carry our good shoes and put them on after we got where we were goin'. One time a whole bunch of us had been to a dance, and your daddy and I walked home down the railroad track. With your daddy and me holdin' hands and him carryin' his fiddle, he couldn't carry my shoes. So Ben carried 'em. It musta been a sight, a man walkin' along behind us carryin' the shoes of the other man's girlfriend!"

I felt sorry for Ben, but I loved hearing Mother tell stories about when she and Daddy were young. And I could tell she was pleased that two men had liked her at the same time, even if she had wanted only one of them.

I had heard Daddy play the same tunes at home, but I had never heard him play for a dance; I'd never even been to one. And I'd never heard people break into applause after Daddy finished a piece like they were doing now. *That's my daddy. Yea, Daddy!*

"Miz Harris?" I looked up and there stood the source of the deep voice: a tall handsome man with dark hair and mustache. Then he asked the question. "Mind if I dance with your little girl?" *Who, me?*

"Oh, that'd be nice, Morton," said Mother. And before I knew it, the man slipped his hands underneath my arms, lifted me off my seat and whisked me down to the floor. Holding one of my hands in his, he whirled me out into the curving line of dancers, the people smiling and the women's skirts swinging when the men twirled them around, all the while keeping time to the music.

"Don't you worry about a thing, little Blondie," said the man Mother called Morton. "I'm gonna take real good care of you." And every time the caller sang out, "Swing your partner," mine lifted me off the floor and swung me high in the air, then put me down again. *Is everybody lookin' at us? Yes, and smilin'.* I was almost too scared for it to be fun, but I was beginning to like it when the music stopped. *Play longer, Daddy. Play longer.*

"Thank you for lendin' me your daughter," said my unsolicited partner when he returned me to Mother's side. "She's a real little lady."

And guess what? I believed him.

First Kiss

The Gibson twins were good-natured boys with identical faces, identical clothing and identical hair every bit as blond as mine. After a few weeks in the second grade with them, I learned to tell them apart. It was a subtle difference, but it was something about the expression around their eyes and mouth. And Mike was a little taller than Mark.

"You can have one, which ever one you want," said Mike one day at recess, stretching out his palm to display a quarter, a dime and a nickel.

I was skeptical. "Is it real money?"

Both boys nodded, their grins a mile wide. "Our mama gives us money. See, I have some, too," said Mark, scratching in his pocket and producing the evidence. *Ooo-eee, I never get that much money!*

"Oh, thank you," I said, reaching for Mike's quarter.

That night, I put the quarter in the shoebox I had stashed underneath my bed to hide my secret treasures.

The next day at school the same thing happened, only this time, it was Mark who offered the money. It didn't matter to me, money was money. And that night, another quarter joined the first one in the shoebox.

The next day, the Gibsons repeated the performance, and the next. School was getting exciting now; I looked forward to going every day.

One night, Mother saw me slip my quarter into the shoebox. "Carole Sue, where'd you get that money?" she asked, puzzled.

"The Gibsons. They gave it to me."

"Well, you can't keep it. You give it back to 'em." *What? You mean I can't keep it?*

"Give it back? Why? I didn't ask for it, they just gave it to me."

"I don't care. Ladies don't take money from men. You take it with you to school tomorrow and tell them I made you give it back and they can't give you any more. And tell them the next time I see their mama, I'm gonna ask her if she knows her boys are givin' away the money she gives 'em." *Why do mothers always spoil everything?*

The next day at recess, in a grassy area between two wings of the school building, I gave the money back. "We didn't mean nothin'," they said, as confused as I was about why we had to stop the game. Then, abruptly, one of the boys—I didn't say which one—pushed me up against the wall and squarely planted his mouth on mine. It was nothing to write home about—just a tight lipped, nose-bumping, dry mouthed kiss-and-run peck, the kisser as wide-eyed in anticipation as I was in surprise. The other twin stood there grinning from ear to ear.

"I'm gonna tell Miz Laura Raye on you," I shouted as they turned and ran.

I didn't. But finally, several days later, I told Mother. "Well, which one was it, Carole Sue?" she asked.

Suddenly, from the look on her face, I knew I should have kept the kiss a secret. "I don't know; I couldn't tell," I lied, completely without malice of forethought.

"Oh. Well, no matter. You just see that you stay with the other girls on the playground from now on. Time enough for boys later."

To their dying day, Mother and Daddy enjoyed telling the story, never varying the ending. "Carole Sue got her first kiss," they laughed, "and doesn't even know who did it!" *Ha! That's what you think!*

As for the twins, neither boy ever admitted the kiss nor implicated the other, nor have I ever revealed the truth. Because we play by the rules: twins never rat on each other, and a lady never kisses and tells.

Surprise Ending

Daddy clicked off the radio. "The war's over," he announced happily. "Let's get all dressed up and go to Washin'ton and see the President." *The war's over? You mean there's not always a war?*

The war had caused the rationing of many consumer goods. Mother saved government-issued coupons for the rationed items, carrying a coupon book in her purse. When she went shopping, she tore out a coupon to give to the merchant, along with money for the purchase. An informal exchange system had grown up around the coupons as people swapped unneeded coupons for needed ones. A meat coupon for a sugar coupon was a bargain to a household with their own livestock but no sugar.

Scarcity of rationed items had resulted in a black market. I didn't know where the black market was, but I knew it was bad to go there. I knew, too, that people who went there paid more money than they would have paid otherwise, but they didn't need coupons. "Black market shoppers—they're awful!" Mother complained. "Actin' like they're better than the people who don't have money to pay extra for somethin' they need. Don't they know that rationin's a way of us helpin' our boys overseas? And the black market operators, they're the lowest of the low, makin' a profit off the war and takin' advantage of desperate people."

She made a point, however, of saving her ration of sugar to bake our birthday cakes. Other than that, we rarely had dessert. Except for Miz Bessie's candy.

Miz Bessie, a widow who lived a couple of miles up the road toward Madisonville, had turned the front room of her house into a small grocery store. Protecting her cotton dress with a white bibbed apron wrapped almost all the way around her ample body, she shuttled back and forth behind the counter, picking off the shelves the items Mother called out to her. "A can of peaches and a loaf of bread—Holsum, please." And Miz Bessie would retrieve the items and place them on the counter in front of Mother, where they waited to be bagged.

Occasionally, Miz Bessie managed to acquire from her supplier a few chocolate bars, scarce items during the war. "I couldn't get much, so I saved it for your kids," she would whisper, tucking the candy into Mother's grocery bag while looking around surreptitiously to see that no one else was watching. The chocolate, sheathed in a metallic gold wrapper, was very dark, very sweet and very good.

"So will we be able to get candy now?" I asked Mother, jumping immediately from Daddy's announcement to the only deprivation I had felt because of the war.

"We'll see." Mother's mind was on something she thought more important than candy. "We're finally at peace! Hallelujah! Mason and Amplis will be comin' home soon. It's what we've all been hopin' and prayin' for."

She had received letters from her brothers, and once she had even opened the cedar chest and showed me the things they had sent her. From his station in North Africa, where he was stationed because his asthma demanded a dry climate, Uncle Amplis had sent a sheer green handkerchief bearing a design of palm trees and camels. From his station in Italy, before he was dispatched to Germany where he would survive the bloody Battle of the Bulge with frozen toes that would later require amputation, Uncle Mason had sent a tiny tin book-like box containing a small white rosary.

"Are we really goin' to see the President?" I thought not, because Washington was really far away. But the ending of a war was something I had never experienced before, and with Mother and Daddy more excited than I'd ever seen them, maybe we really would go to see the President.

"Well, go get ready and see," said Mother as she began laying out the clothes John and I would wear on the trip.

I looked up to see John rolling his eyes. I didn't like it when he thought he was my boss, but I liked it when he gave me clues. *No, we're not goin' to Washin'ton to see the President; we're just goin' to Madisonville. I'm the littlest, and they always try to fool me.*

The sidewalks of Madisonville were full of people in spontaneous victory celebration. Men clapped each other on the back and women alternately laughed and cried. People hung halfway out the open windows of passing cars and beat on the doors, yelling, "It's over, it's over! Yea, the war's over!" The policeman at the intersection of Main and Center Streets repeatedly blew his traffic whistle in merriment as everybody excitedly speculated on how soon "the boys" would be home.

But what I remember most is how astonished I was that war was not a part of the natural order, like the sun coming up and going down. And when the war ended, it was a surprise ending.

A Full Moon

Mother spread the ratty old blanket on the kitchen floor and set a washtub on the blanket. It was a daily ritual. As soon as Daddy came home from the mine, Mother spread out the blanket, filled the tub with four or five inches of water, and heated Daddy's bath by pouring into it boiling water heated on the kitchen range.

Dropping his bib overalls down to the waist, Daddy removed his shirt and undershirt, knelt on the blanket facing the tub, leaned forward and splashed warm water on his face, head and neck. Rubbing them and his hands with a bar of soap, he splashed on more water to rinse off the lather. Small streams running down his forearms and dripping off his bent elbows onto the blanket, the soapy rivulets left tiny white streaks on his coal-blackened arms.

For some things, once is not enough. One of those things is washing a coal miner's face. With coal dust rimming his eyes and embedded at the base of his eyelashes, Daddy repeated the soaping-splashing process two or three times until Mother pronounced his face clean.

"Okay, you kids. Out!" Daddy said.

If it had been summer, John and I would have been outside already. But it was winter, so our retreat was the living room, which was unheated to conserve fuel. For as much coal as the mine loaded every day and as near as we were to the mine, Daddy purchased our coal and had a dump truck deliver it, just like the people in Madisonville did. And since Mother and Daddy were saving money to buy a house in town, we didn't heat a room if we would use it for only a few minutes.

"How come Mother gets to stay in the kitchen when you take your bath and we don't?" I asked Daddy.

Seizing the initiative, Mother answered for him. "So I can wash his back." *Uh-oh, Mother thinks Daddy will say the wrong thing.*

"But I mean, how come it's all *right* for you to stay in and it's not all right for us?"

"Because we're married, that's why! Don't ask so many questions." *Oh. So you don't want to say why.*

Wordlessly, John and I retreated to the living room. *Hurry up, Daddy, it's cold in here.* Soon I lost patience. *I know what I'll do. I'll go to the bedroom and get one of my books.* The trip to the bedroom and the search for the book creating just enough distraction for me to fall into habit when I left the room, I opened the kitchen door by mistake. And there stood Daddy, his wholly unadorned profile bending over the tub.

In the split second that he turned toward the sound of the opening door, I slammed it shut and ran. And believe it or not, the only thing

I really saw was the shock on Daddy's face when his startled eyes met my horrified ones.

Gratefully, Daddy never mentioned the incident of the full moon. And never, until now, did I.

Guardian Angel

The strip mine had done its job and abandoned its destructive ugliness. Left on the Parham property were a 25-foot high spoil bank and a deep drainage ditch about 15 feet wide, the repository of the inevitable storm water that raced unimpeded down the sides of the gigantic mound of bare earth. Eroding trenches in the side of the embankment, the storm water and its collected sediment spilled into the ditch, where the pollution flowed into the nearby stream, contaminating it and filling it up with silt.

When people destroy the earth, they destroy themselves, said Franklin D. Roosevelt. Eventually, reclamation efforts would smooth down west Kentucky's stripped areas and convert them to a useful purpose or return them to their approximate original appearance, the topsoil restored and planted in native grasses and ground cover. Largely unrecognizable today as formerly active mining areas, these reclaimed areas host parks, lakes, trails, pastures or productive farmland.

But in 1940s west Kentucky, reclamation of strip mine areas was a thing of the future. It was common to see abandoned spoil banks rising high against the sky, a few small eruptions of fire burning for years on the sides of the banks. Spewing out a small stream of continuous smoke and an occasional flickering flame, the result of the spontaneous combustion of coal residues compressed underneath tons of earth, the mini-flames filled the air with an omnipresent sulfurous odor. If the people in coal country discussed the relative merits of strip mining, debated whether it constituted a rape of the land or an appropriate use of natural resources that lifted many families out of poverty, I have no memory of it. Coal mining, underground or strip, was life—simply life.

John and I, along with the three Harper kids, walked up to the Parham house, vacant since our family moved out. Standing on the bank of the drainage ditch behind the barn, we didn't know that we were standing on the brink of danger.

Wading into the water in their jeans and tee shirts, the two taller and more adventurous girls made their slippery way to the middle. There they stood, splashing their arms in water deep enough to cover their shoulders and surveying the three of us standing on the bank. None of us could swim.

"C'mon, Carole Sue," motioned Marilyn, spotting a derelict fence post floating nearby. "We'll float you on the log." *Mother says never to get in the water. But I won't be in the water; I'll be on the log.* Joyce coaxing me, I removed my shoes and socks and rolled my jeans up above my knees. Straddling the post, I slid to the center as the two girls held my makeshift transport stationary. After I solidly seated myself, legs dangling in the water up to my knees, the girls towed the poor excuse for a log out to the middle and gave it a downstream shove. "This'll be the ride of your life," shouted Joyce.

Indeed! My weight instantly spun the post in the water and rotated me to the underside, completely immersing me. Down, down I swirled in the dark, losing my grip on the post, my nasal passages screaming in pain from inhaled water. *Lord, help!* Suddenly, my neck jerked violently backward as Joyce grabbed a handful of hair. Abruptly yanked into daylight, I splashed frantically into the grappling arms of the two older girls—my third childhood victory over the risks of life in coal country.

Tugging me out onto the ground, the kids slapped me on the back as I coughed and sputtered, spitting out mouthfuls of muddy water.

When I finally stopped crying, my frightened friends inspected me. My head had scraped the bottom of the ditch, caking my hair with mud, and the shin of my right leg was bleeding from a snag on an exposed nail, a straggler left behind in the post from the days it actually served as a fence.

"We gotta get her cleaned up," Marilyn said. Splashing me with water from the drainage ditch, the other kids used their cupped hands to pour more water on my hair, washing away the mud. Then they "cleaned" the cut on my shin with more dirty water.

Walking me across the meadow to the back of the barn, they removed my tee shirt and jeans and stretched them out in the sun, then instructed me to sit in the sun until my underwear and hair were dry. Later in the afternoon, the three Harpers swore both John and me to secrecy about what had happened. *Tell? Do you think I'm crazy? Mother will kill me again, and John, too, for lettin' me get in the water in the first place.*

"Ca-role Soo-oo!" cried Mother, aborting her tuneless whistle, her stricken face telegraphing her horror the very second John and I walked into the house. "What in the world happened to you?" *How does she always know?*

I burst into tears.

Confronted, John told the story as Mother consoled me. Then she gently bathed me and shampooed my hair, lightly smoothed lotion on my sunburned skin, swabbed my wound with disinfectant and applied a clean gauze bandage. Dressing me in one of Daddy's soft tee shirts, she tucked me into bed, the cool sheets as welcome as warm hugs.

Mother hadn't been tipped off just because my hair was dirty, she told Daddy later. My formerly white tee shirt had been stained muddy beige and I was wearing it label side out. And my jeans, which I always wore rolled up to mid-calf in the style of the day, had been rolled down to hide the cut on my leg. "We moved to get the kids away from that dangerous place, and now look what happened!" Mother exclaimed. "Merciful God! He musta sent a guardian angel to look after this kid; otherwise, she'd be dead." Rainbow mercy, even without the rainbow!

Mother was merciful, too. She knew that mothers don't kill kids who've already been scared to death.

Five. Rainbow Truth

Rainbow arch . . . whose light is truth. . .[5]

— Oliver Wendell Holmes

Message Needed

"P-o-n-e-y." I raced through the letters, then—*Ow! No 'e.'*
'Pony' has no 'e' in it! Why did I say that?
I had already spelled harder words than "pony" that afternoon,
and had spelled down everybody else in the class except Janie
Renford. She, one of the Gibson boys, or I usually won the spelling
bee, a regular Friday afternoon feature of the third grade. The
friendly competition was designed to review the words the class had
learned in our daily reading assignments.

"No," said Miz Phelps.

*You were goin' too fast, girl. Slow down and think before you
speak!* The other kids were already in their seats, watching and
waiting. *Don't look at me like that! If you could spell 'pony,' you
wouldn't be sittin' down!*

The expressionless face below Miz Phelps' dark bangs, which she
wore in what Mother called a 1920s finger wave, was unreadable.
She was a good teacher and I got along well with her, but I preferred
my teachers predictable, especially when I made a mistake. Still, I
was in my second year at Anton school, and I had yet to see or hear
of a teacher whipping a student, so I was a little less worried about
making a mistake now than I had been last year.

Miz Phelps turned her expressionless eyes on my friend. "Spell
pony, Janie."

"P-o-n-y."

"Right."

I knew Janie could spell pony, especially now that she knew how
not to spell it. But to win the bee, she would have to spell correctly

not just the word I had missed, but the next word Miz Phelps would give her. If Janie misspelled that word, I would be back in the contest. *Maybe Janie will miss the next word and I'll get another chance.*

"Cowboy," said Miz Phelps.

Cowboy? Everybody knows how to spell 'cowboy.' You just spell 'cow' and 'boy' and put 'em together. My heart sank.

"C-o-w-b-o-y," spelled Janie. No hesitation, no "uh" to buy time for thinking, no frowning with eyes turned up toward the ceiling in an unconscious attempt to pull out of the mind something buried deep within it.

"Right," said Miz Phelps. "Janie's the winner today." *Oh, no, I* raged at myself. *That's what I get for goin' too fast!*

That night, Mother listened to my sad tale as we washed and dried the supper dishes. She was unsympathetic. "Your mistake wasn't in goin' too fast,'" said Mother. "Your mistake was in under-estimatin' the competition. You're not the *only* one who can spell, ya'know."

Message needed, message heeded.

Show and Tell

Mother was ready to close the cedar chest after placing something inside it. "Let me see, let me see," I begged. "I wanna see!"

"Not now; I'm busy." Lowering the lid and locking it, she pocketed the key and went off to do whatever she was doing. *'Not now' sometimes means 'never,' only she doesn't want to say it. But sometimes it means 'maybe later.'*

Later that day, I asked again. "Oh, all right," she said. "We'll take a look. But you have to go into the other room so I can get the key." *She's never gonna let me see where she keeps the key!* But I did as she asked. Minutes later she called me, and when I went back into the bedroom, she had pulled two chairs up beside the cedar chest and already had the lid up.

Everything Mother showed me had a story to go with it. The potbellied doll wearing the purple dress with cream lace trim had been hers when she was a little girl. The marble of golf ball size with the multi-colored swirls had been a gift from Santa Claus when Mother was little. The cigar box full of buttons and loose beads had belonged to Great-Grandma Sisk, who had let Mother play with them when she was a child. Two or three rings, their circles broken but the stones still intact, had belonged to Grandma Sisk when she was young.

Mary Jane and Overall Bill had been saved because John and I would appreciate them when we were grown. *The Story of Jesus,* a preschool book, had my name written inside in Mother's hand. John's and my birth certificates accompanied a baby book for each of us. *She wrote all that stuff down in a book—our birth weights, our first words, the dates of our first steps and all that? You mean she knows all that stuff?*

A tiny pink wooden clothes hanger had once held my baby dresses. The small cuttings of blond hair, each tied with a tiny blue ribbon, had been snipped and dated on my birthday each year. One of the baby dresses had been mine, the other had been John's, and the same for the two pairs of baby shoes. Two little white boxes held the baby teeth extracted from our mouths. The tiny gold St. Christopher medal on a brass safety pin had been a gift from a Catholic friend to the baby who now slept with a little granite lamb. The pressed rose in the small white Bible had come from the floral wreath that covered the baby's casket.

Show-and-tell time was finally over. Mother closed the cedar chest and locked the lid. "This'll all be yours someday," she said, her eyes moist.

It was a promise I remembered. But remembrance is not the same as acceptance, and to me, the cedar chest would always belong to Mother. And I would always need her permission to see inside it.

Kiss the Horse

What Mother and Daddy did when we went to Madisonville on Saturday afternoon, I have no idea. But whatever it was, they did it while John and I went to a movie. Occasionally, if they didn't have too much to do, they'd go with us.

Besides a preview of upcoming movies, an episode of an adventure serial preceded the movie. Running about 12 episodes of about 15 minutes each, all segments except the final one ended in a cliffhanger with the hero—a cowboy, a knight or a superhero comic book character—in peril. It was a transparent ploy to keep people coming back every Saturday. It worked. John and I tried never to miss an episode, and if for some reason we did, our first duty the next day at Sunday school was to find a friend who could tell us what had happened the day before.

And there was always at least one color cartoon. It might be Bugs Bunny, Mickey Mouse, the Roadrunner, Porky Pig, Tom and Jerry or some other popular animal character. Whichever the character, I hated the violence. One of the more common incidents was a fall or a push off a high cliff, the victim landing flat as a pancake on the ground below, then miraculously turning on edge and rolling off like a wheel. *Why is it okay to laugh when an animal gets hurt?* I never learned the answer.

The black and white movie itself was a Western. Roy Rogers and Dale Evans were popular. So were Gene Autry, the Lone Ranger, Tex Ritter, the Durango Kid and Hopalong Cassidy. The formula was predictable. Cowboys were always brave. Indians were always wise. The pretty woman was always helpless. And always, at the end of the movie, the cowboy—except for Roy Rogers, who was married to Dale Evans in real life—straddled his horse and rode off without the woman.

"Why does the man always kiss the horse instead of the woman?" pondered Daddy one day. *Oh, Daddy, don't be silly. The cowboy never kisses the horse!*

"Because he's never kissed me, I guess," replied Mother, giving Daddy a sideways glance.

It was a period of innocence in filmmaking, an innocence matched by my own. For I had no idea what Mother had insinuated.

A Full Load

Before we piled into our sedan to return home from Madisonville that Saturday, Daddy removed the back seat and stowed it diagonally in the trunk. Too long to fit the space, the seat extended out over the rear bumper at least a foot. Resting the edge of the trunk lid on the seat, Daddy tied the lid down with a rope and stashed the family purchase of the day in the area behind the front seat where the back seat had been. Then he put me up front in Mother's lap and squeezed John into the middle of the front seat between himself and Mother, the stick shift on the floorboard rising between John's knees as we rode home.

"Oh, no, there's Dickie Durwood goin' home," said Mother, spotting the back of the familiar lumbering form ahead of us in his bib overalls. Dickie's slue-footed walk was unmistakable, even from the rear.

"Dickie's a good man," people said, "but he's a little slow. He'll probably always live with his mama and daddy." Every Saturday, Dickie walked to Madisonville to pass the time of day with the other men sitting underneath the Tree of Knowledge, the treed perimeter lined with park benches around the Hopkins County Courthouse. After a couple of hours, he ambled across Main Street to Woolworth's dime store and purchased a comic book with money he had earned helping his daddy work their farm. The comic book would be Dickie's reading companion on the walk home.

"But I've got to at least stop," said Daddy. "He knows our car."

"No," argued Mother, "there's no place to put him."

"I know. But he'll have to see that, otherwise, he'll never understand. We can't hurt his feelin's."

By now we had passed Dickie. Daddy braked the car and slowly pulled to a halt on the side of the road 50 yards or so in front of the ungainly man.

"Hey, Dickie," yelled Daddy, sticking his head out the driver's window and waving.

"Hey, Sterlin'," yelled Dickie, quickening his step to reach the car.

"I'd give you a ride, Dickie, but as you can see, I've got a full load today."

"That's okay," said Dickie, peering through the window, then opening the back door and seating himself on the floorboard. "I don't mind if they don't."

After Daddy got us back on the road, I glanced back over Mother's shoulder at Dickie and his familiar infectious grin. There he sat, an arm flung around the neck of one of the hogs, the other hog resting on its haunches between Dickie's sprawled legs.

"I guess they didn't mind," laughed Daddy after he let Dickie out in front of his house. "They didn't say nothin'."

We had carried a full load that day, and some people said Dickie never would. But he was an accepted member of the community and he carried all he could. Which is exactly what we did.

Reading the Flame

Daddy sat at the kitchen table with his safety lamp. A stainless steel and glass cylinder, it was about ten inches high and four inches in diameter. With its blaze glowing inside a transparent hollow glass tube fixed at the top and bottom between layers of steel wire gauze that covered all the openings and prevented the flame from igniting any gas encountered underground, it was the only flame allowed in the mine. Smokers had to wait until they were above ground before lighting up.

Disassembling the lamp and carefully inspecting the parts, Daddy laid them out in a row on the table. Then, picking them up one by one, he polished each piece with a soft cloth to remove the accumulated coal residues that had gradually filtered through the fittings during daily use.

"What are you doin', Daddy?"

"Makin' sure my lamp works right, Sis," said Daddy, calling me the name he used when mentioning me to John. "I could be in bad trouble if it fails." After each piece met Daddy's approval, he meticulously reassembled them and held the lamp up toward the bare electric light bulb swinging overhead, as though admiring an expensive piece of jewelry. "Now!" he said with finality, the monosyllable signaling his satisfaction with his work.

In charge of mine safety, Daddy was the only miner I'd ever seen exit the cage carrying a safety lamp. Sometimes it was in his hand, and sometimes it swung from a hook on his belt opposite the battery that powered his headlamp.

The safety lamp fascinated me—the sparkle of its glass, the burnished shine of its metal, the symmetrical beauty of its shape and the mild clack it made as it gently bounced against the brads in Daddy's overalls when he strode through the front door into the house. The clack was the perfect complement for the soft whisper of Daddy's denim-covered legs brushing against one another—swoosh, swoosh—as he made his way through the living room to the kitchen, where he sat down on a wooden chair, untied his shoes and dropped them on the floor.

"How does it work, Daddy?"

"It burns a different flame when it detects methane or black damp in the mine." Methane, a potentially explosive gas formed by decaying vegetative matter, is kept within safe limits in underground mines by a ventilation system comprised chiefly of gigantic fans that blow air inside and draw it out, circulating it throughout the tunnels and working areas. Black damp, strictly speaking, is deadly carbon dioxide, but the term also describes an atmosphere depleted of oxygen.

"But how does that help?"

"Because I know how to read the flame, sorta like readin' a book to learn what to do about somethin'." *Oh.*

"Like doin' what?"

"Like crankin' up the ventilation fans a notch or two to increase the flow of fresh air underground, or hangin' up a curtain to redirect the flow of air. Or sealin' off an area of the mine so the air won't have to cover as much territory. Or maybe spreadin' rock dust around everywhere so the coal dust won't catch fire from a stray electrical spark or spontaneous combustion." *Spontaneous combustion?*

Giving the lamp a gentle swipe with his shirtsleeve, Daddy brushed off an imaginary piece of lint, obviously finished with the discussion. "This is my insurance," he said, rising from his chair and setting the lamp beside the door so he could easily find his gear the next morning.

It was an appropriate term. Insurance is a tool you keep in hope that you'll never need it.

Papaws and Persimmons

"Looks like a papaw-pickin' day to me," said Mother, pulling one of Daddy's long-sleeved shirts on over her dress. "Let's go before the sun gets too hot."

"Papaws?" I asked. "What's a papaw?"

"You'll see. Put your jeans on and one of your long-sleeved shirts so the blackberry briars won't scratch you. We're goin' papaw pickin'."

Oh, the blackberry bushes. I knew they were in the thicket alongside the road between our house and the mine. We had been there before to pick the wild berries Mother baked in the cobblers that I liked better than regular pies because of the cobblers' juiciness. And because of the grainy sugar Mother sprinkled on the buttery top crust to brown in the oven.

I was dressed and ready to go in two minutes.

Zigzagging her way through the underbrush, Mother was about two steps ahead of me. "Here they are," she said, pointing out the tropical-like leaves providing a mid-story layer in that area of the thicket. Fruitless on my other trips to the grove, the small papaw trees had always escaped my attention, scant competition as they were for the pretentious flowering dogwoods that shouted in the spring, "Look at me, look at me," and the mimosas with their spidery pink blossoms that lasted way up into the summer.

"Looks like most of 'em are about ripe," Mother said, reaching to pluck one of the oblong banana-curved yellow fruits about four inches long. "See how the skin is gettin' little brown spots on it, like a ripe banana? But the skin is not as thick as a banana's, and you can eat it if you want to."

When we took the papaws home and washed them, I was delighted with the taste. Sweet, aromatic and juicier than a banana, the best part of the flesh was the custard-like pulp surrounding the smooth, flat brown inch-long seeds inside. *The seeds look sorta like a persimmon seed.*

The year before, the persimmon tree on the lane leading from the Harper's house to the access road for the mine had gotten the best of me. How well I remember the day I lost my patience waiting for the persimmons to ripen! Having gazed longingly at the loaded tree until my curiosity got the better of my judgment, I plucked one of the spherical fruits about an inch in diameter.

As pretty as it was, the flesh of the unripe persimmon filled my entire oral cavity with an astringent tissue-coating, eye-squinting, face-puckering mealy film. No one makes that mistake more than once! Immediately regretting my folly, I thereafter waited until the smooth amber fruit had turned a deep orange. The flat oblong seeds were the only leftovers, the juicy fruit a sweet reward for waiting.

Papaws and persimmons. Not all of the natural resources in coal country were underground.

Country Road

"Let's all walk up to Miz Bessie's," suggested John. All of the neighbor kids were playing in our front yard that summer day. The Yorks had moved away and the Burdens had moved into the vacant house, adding Virginia Mae to the three Harpers, John and me. Now there were six kids to make the walk: two boys and four girls. On rare occasions in the summer, our mothers permitted this group excursion that took almost all day to accomplish.

First came the heavy negotiating. We had to get three mothers to agree that the weather wasn't too hot for the trek and that it wouldn't rain before we got back. Then we had to get permission. That meant numerous trips back and forth to each other's houses to reassure each mother that the other mothers had authorized the trip. Then we had to persuade the mothers to give us money to buy candy, and then we had to walk all the way to Miz Bessie's and back. It was a chore!

Miz Bessie liked John and me, and we knew it because of the candy she had saved for us during the war. But I also knew it because of the feed sacks. A 100-pound chicken feed sack, made from a coarse cotton floral or geometric print, was enough fabric for Mother to make a dress for me, and Miz Bessie always saved her feed sacks for Mother. By now, Mother owned a treadle sewing machine, and she made most of my clothes.

To get to the store, we walked down the road to the school bus stop and turned north, walked past the mining camp, crossed the bridge over the creek, and went past the Durwood's house. Finally, we reached Miz Bessie's store.

The best part about the trip wasn't the candy we bought once we arrived at the store, but the trip itself. We lollygagged and chit-chatted, stopping along the way to pick a few blossoms off the fragrant honeysuckles blooming against the fencerows beside the road. Pulling the yellowish white blooms apart, we licked off the sweet drop of nectar at the base of the flowers. And we picked up the 15-inch long inedible bean pods littering the ground underneath a tall catalpa tree, using the pods to conduct a coal country version of a sword fight.

We skipped flat rocks in the creek, then took our shoes off and waded in the stream, the water just barely high enough to flow softly across our feet. Once, we even climbed the Durwoods' fence and picked up some apples underneath the trees in their small orchard. It wasn't stealing, we reassured each other. We knew that Mr. Durwood would give us the apples if we asked, but it was more fun to climb the fence and skulk around in the orchard than to knock on the door and ask for the apples.

And when we were lucky enough to get permission for a fall trip on a rare day off from school, we gathered the black walnuts and hickory nuts that fell on the road, taking our find home and cracking the nuts on the hearth with a hammer before picking out the crunchy nutmeats inside.

"Remember who you are," warned John, clutching my elbow when we approached Miz Bessie's store. It was his customary way of reminding me that I was a part of a family with high standards for our behavior. *I know, I know. Why does he say stuff like that?*

Because he was the eldest child in the same family, that's why. It was a part of leading the way.

Down on the Farm

It was my week at Grandma and Grandpa Sisk's farm—or rather, at the farm they tenanted for Elmer Ward. Nobody in our family had ever owned anything except the clothes on our backs, a few sticks of furniture, and a rattly old car.

Grandma and Grandpa were polar opposites, for Grandpa was rail thin and Grandma was—not. In fact, they could have been the model for nursery rhyme's Mr. and Miz Jack Spratt: he could eat no fat and she could eat no lean.

Betty Sue was at the farm, too. Two kids would be less trouble for Grandma than one because we would entertain each other, Mother said. And entertain ourselves we did, with the help of Grandma's mechanical Victrola and its wind-up crank, revolving turntable and quarter-inch thick records.

The best part about playing the Victrola was turning the crank until it was very tight. When we stopped cranking, the records spun so fast that the singer's voices rose high pitched and chirpy. Giggling, Betty and I sat on the floor and mocked the vocalists, waiting for the mechanism to unwind until the records spun so slowly that the voices sounded very low and very slow.

Afterwards, Grandma taught us nonsensical songs—ditties, she called them—clapping her hands and laughing with us as we sang.

Ee-quack monie, monie, monie, monie oss-ko
Ee-quack quoo, ee-quack quoh.
Oh Nick-o-deem-o, oh Charlie-arlie om-o,
Oh Nick-o-deem-o, oh Charlie-arlie,
Oom-phah, oom-phah, ooo-phah.

Grandpa kept a few dairy cows, and sometimes Grandma let Betty and me make butter, taking turns pumping the round wooden dasher up and down inside the tall milk-filled crockery churn until our arms became so tired that we had to stop for rest. And sometimes Grandma sent us to the hen house to collect the brown eggs from the hens' nests, or to the garden to pick the juicy red tomatoes and crisp green cucumbers she would serve at supper. Sliced thinly and combined with circles of sliced sweet onions, then sprinkled with black pepper, the vegetable trio marinated in cider vinegar until Grandma dished them up in small individual bowls. The combination comprised a frequent summer salad.

All grandpas are special, but mine was special and wise. "You can be the best if you wanna be," he told me once. "Because most people don't do their best. So all you gotta do to be the best is do *your* best more often than they do."

A riddle often preceded Grandpa's lessons. "If a man picked up a calf the first day it was born, and then picked it up every day thereafter while the calf was gettin' heavier and the man was gettin' stronger, would the man still be able to pick up the cow after it was grown?"

I knew the answer was no, but it seemed like it should be yes. But then, that didn't seem right, either. "I don't know, Grandpa. Would he?"

"No. Because, ya' see, the way the question's asked, it makes you think the problem is how much the calf weighs. But that's not all there is to it. It's also how big the calf is and how much it cooperates."

"Oh, Grandpa, you and your riddles!" I laughed.

Then, in a response good enough for Management 101, he said, "Well, ya'see, sometimes the real problem's not what it seems like it is. So first, you gotta figure out what the problem is before you start to figure out the answer."

Nights, because Grandpa was illiterate but loved the written word, perhaps more than people who could read, Betty Sue and I sat quietly on the floor by the light of the kerosene lamp while Grandma read *The Madisonville Messenger* aloud to Grandpa. More than the words, I remember the steady drone of Grandma's voice as Grandpa smoked the cigarettes he hand rolled from the small drawstring bag of loose tobacco and cigarette papers stashed in his shirt pocket, his rocking chair swaying slowly back and forth, lightly squeaking.

When Betty and I started to yawn, Grandma ushered us to bed in the room next to hers and Grandpa's. Sinking into the comfort of a homemade straw mattress, Betty and I watched the shadows dance on the floor, the ballet of moonlight filtered through lightly stirring lace curtains. With the distant rasp of tree crickets wafting through the open window on honeysuckle-scented breezes, we drifted to sleep on the airy wings of nature's night music.

Only 12 miles from the clanking rattle of a working coal mine and the sulfurous odor of burning spoil banks, the world down on the farm was a world almost too idyllic to be real.

It was real. But nothing lasts forever, and the farm was a reality that would not last long.

The Price of Meat

It was breakfast time on a wintry hog-killing day at the farm, and I was the only grandchild there this time. Grandpa had given me a cup of sassafras tea with a teaspoonful of honey added. Brewed from the red roots of a sassafras tree, the clear caffeine-free hot tea was a lovely cold weather beverage, especially for people who didn't like coffee. Granddaddy didn't.

Hog killing was a once-a-year event that always occurred on a very cold day. With no refrigeration, working outside in the cold was the only means available to protect the meat from spoiling as the farmer processed it. For this labor-intensive occasion in which a massive amount of work took place as quickly as possible, neighbors always gathered to help. It was an unspoken agreement: the favor would be returned when hog-killing day arrived at their farm.

I knew a little about the work involved, because our family had helped the Strongs on hog-killing day, adding our two hogs to theirs. I had hung out in the kitchen with the women as they made lunch for the men, ground the fresh sausage, seasoned it with sage and black pepper, and packed it into cloth rolls.

After finishing his meal of pan-fried bacon and eggs, hot buttered biscuits, homemade blackberry jam and sassafras tea, Grandpa pulled on his heavy coat and left for the hog pen, clearly expecting me to stay with Grandma and the other women now arriving for work. *I'm not stayin' in the kitchen this time!*

"Grandma," I announced, "I'm goin' to the hog pen with Granddaddy."

"No, you stay here," she said. "Morgan don't want you getting' in the way." *What's she talkin' about? Grandpa knows I won't get in the way!* Grabbing my coat when Grandma wasn't looking, I sneaked out the back door and crept behind the barn to the hog pen, where I climbed the fence and seated myself on the top rail.

Several men were milling around in the hog pen with Grandpa when he picked up a club and began to circle one of the hogs. *Oh, no!* Immediately, I realized two things: Grandpa intended to use the club on the hog, and I didn't want to see it. Until that moment, "hog killin'" had simply been a term without meaning. Too late, it was too real. Quickly, I turned away.

Swoosh! Club through air. Thwack! Club against skull. *It's over.* Turning around, I was just in time to see Grandpa toss the club aside in favor of a long butcher knife. *Oh, no! It's not over!* One quick thrust of the knife and the downed hog's blood gushed out onto the ground, her legs quivering convulsively in midair.

Someone screamed—was it I?—as visible waves of undulating revulsion streamed in front of my eyes and lapped against the shoals of my horror, waxing and waning, surging and retreating in an insane struggle to shield my innocence from the repulsive ordinariness of routine slaughter.

Just then, Grandpa looked up and spotted me perched on the fence. "Grandma Della was supposed to keep you at home," he said helplessly, averting his eyes. I jumped from the fence and ran to the house.

Mother often complained about the price of meat. I don't think this is what she meant.

Runaway

Bouncing up and down, I gripped the wagon seat with both hands. *I begged to come; I can't let him know I don't like it.*

At first, it had been fun going for a wagon ride with Grandpa. But when we topped the hill and started down, the pair of horses began to race faster and faster, and fun became fright.

Grandpa stood up and pulled back on the reins. "Whoa! Whoa!" he shouted. But the ground underneath the horses' feet continued to fly, the creaky wagon rattling louder and louder as we bounced along the bumpy road. *It's a runaway, just like in a Western movie!*

Bracing his feet against the front wall of the wagon, Grandpa tightly gripped the reins and leaned back in a futile effort to use the leverage of his slightly built body to rein in the horses. "Whoa!" he shouted, "Whoa!" Racing horses and rickety wagon wildly rumbling onto level ground at the foot of the hill, they slowed and finally stopped, the horses wet with sweat and their breath coming in quick huffs.

Grandpa reached into his back pocket, pulled out his red bandana and wiped his brow. "Whew!" he breathed, dropping to the wagon seat winded, his face ashen underneath his day's growth of gray beard.

"What happened, Grandpa?"

"I lost control of the horses. It wasn't their fault, they're good horses. I don't know exactly what happened; we've been down this hill lotsa times. We musta been goin' faster than I thought when we crested the top."

We slowly rolled home, where we put the horses out to pasture before we went to the well. Drawing a bucket of water, Grandpa reached for the hollowed-out gourd hanging among the morning glories climbing the scaffold for the rope pulley and metal bucket. Dipping the gourd into the bucket, Grandpa gave me a sip of the distinctly flavored water, woody tasting from its contact with the gourd. Then, bringing the gourd to his lips, he drank deeply, the water trickling down one corner of his mouth and dripping off his chin. Swiping the trickle with the back of his hand, Grandpa hung the gourd back in place, took a few strides toward the back porch and sank down on the steps.

I gathered up my skirt and sat down beside him. "Put your hand here and feel," Grandpa said, sliding my hand between the bib of his overalls and the shirt underneath it. "Feel that?"

"Uh-huh." I had felt my own throbbing heartbeat, so I knew what to expect. But there was something else I didn't expect: a noticeable bulge in the wall of his chest. "How come there's a hump in your chest?"

"Enlarged heart," said Granddaddy. "My ribs have expanded to give it room. Doctor says I have heart failure and I need to stop workin' so hard. I think maybe he's right."

Indeed he was, and Grandpa and Grandma soon opted for an apartment in Madisonville, leaving the farm to my memories. I would continue my regular visits to their home, though, and at age 15, I would sit quietly alone by Grandpa's bedside as his failing heart finally stopped beating.

Grandpa was less scared that day than on the day the horses ran away. In fact, we both were.

Getting Nowhere

By the time I realized I shouldn't have come, it was too late.

Having arrived early at the school bus stop with the other kids from Bosses Row, I left them at the rough wooden shelter and walked up the road a short distance to Barbara Jarrett's house, where I knocked on the front door. *I'll be warmer inside Barbara's house waitin' for the bus than standin' inside the bus shelter.* From the Jarretts' front window, Barbara and I would be able to see the bus coming, and we would have plenty of time to run from the house to the bus stop by the time the bus arrived.

Barbara and three of her younger brothers lived with their parents in one of the camp houses, a row of several faded barn-red houses belonging to Pine Hill coal mine. The houses, even smaller and more poorly constructed than ours, were too far from the mine to have electrical wiring, and they sheltered families headed by men with the lowest paying jobs in the mine.

"Come in," said Miz Jarrett, opening the door. "Barbara'll be through in a minute. She's jes' now finishin' up her readin' homework." *Why is Barbara just now doin' her homework?* John and I did our homework when we first got home from school so we could get to our free time playing games or reading *Piggly Wiggly, Lassie Come Home* and other books we thought more interesting than our textbooks.

The Jarretts' house was smelly. Leftover food scraps for the dog littered the grimy bare floor and soiled clothes cluttered the few pieces of dilapidated furniture in the room that served as both living room and kitchen. Dirty pans containing leftover food from the night before sat stacked on the back of the coal range, oatmeal-encrusted cereal bowls randomly strewn about the kitchen table. The most recent runny-nosed baby lay crying in the background. *Poor little thing, wonder what's wrong with him?*

Miz Jarrett's weak smile flashed her rotting teeth. Her faded grease-spotted cotton dress hanging loosely on her stoop-shouldered frame, she was the epitome of poverty's inadequate nutrition and poor hygiene. Motioning me toward the broken-down sofa, she sat down on one end as I sat on the other, Barbara between us.

One of the weakest readers in the third grade, Barbara started reading aloud, Miz Jarrett supplying words as needed. *Uh-oh! Miz Jarrett can't read much better than Barbara.* Suddenly, for reasons I didn't understand, I felt very uncomfortable. *I shouldn't have come.*

Struggling with a word, Barbara came to a halt and waited for a prompt. "N-o-w-h-e-r-e," mouthed Miz Jarrett silently. Coming to a decision, she announced it. "Now here," she said hesitantly.

Oh, no, she's tellin' Barbara wrong. "Nowhere," I blurted out.

"Nowhere," repeated Miz Jarrett softly, lowering her eyes. *Oh, no. I shouldn't have said that. I'm not supposed to know more than a grownup knows. And if I do, I'm not supposed to show it.*

At least as embarrassed as Miz Jarrett was, I grabbed my books and darted for the door. "C'mon, Barbara," I said. "The bus'll be here in a minute."

Everybody gets nowhere sometime. But the day I got nowhere, I saw the rainbow light of truth: Sometimes it's better to be kind than to be right.

Six. Rainbow Wonder

The rainbow arching over in the skies,
New sparks of wonder opening in surprise. . .[6]

— D. H. Lawrence

Power Play

It was exciting and more than a little scary. Through a process unknown to me, the high school students had selected me for a small role in their Christmas drama. The play would be at night, my fourth grade teacher had told me, and grownups would be there, along with students from all the other classes. *Ooo-eee, a real play, not a little kid thing!*

The only elementary-age child in the play, I would be inside a big gift box on stage near the Christmas tree. When I heard my cue, I would burst out of the box in a red dress, stretch out my arms and say, "And a red dress, too!"

That's it; that's all I had to do—except tell Mother about the red dress. Which I promptly forgot about.

One Saturday night after we came home from a trip to Madisonville, Mother opened a paper bag from J.C. Penney's. "Look at the new dress I got for you to wear in the Christmas play," she said, holding up a navy blue sailor dress with gold buttons, a red tie and a white square collar edged with gold piping. *A store-bought dress, not even homemade. But—*

"But I'm supposed to wear a red dress," I wailed.

"Oh. Well, I don't think you told me that," said Mother indifferently. "You'll just have to tell Miz Larkin I didn't know you were supposed to wear a red dress, and you haven't got one." *Oh, no! I'm gonna be in a real play and I've got the wrong color dress! Miz Larkin will take my part away and give it to somebody with a red dress!*

135

My fourth grade teacher, Mother and Daddy had said, was divorced—the only divorced person I knew. "She can't help it," Mother had said. "Her husband ran off and left her, and his two kids, too. What a scoundrel!" *No wonder Miz Larkin looks sad.* "She'll be all right, though," said Mother. "She's got an education. She'll be able to support herself and the kids. That's why you've gotta stay in school, so you can take care of yourself if you ever have to. Things happen. You can't ever tell. You gotta be able to earn a livin'."

The next day, I laid my problem on the frail shoulders of my teacher, a tall thin woman with sad eyes and stringy brown hair pulled back with combs behind her ears. Fixing her eyes on the paper in her bony hands, Miz Larkin didn't look up. "Oh," she said insipidly, the veins in the backs of her hands standing up blue and puffy like the veins on her inside ankles. "Well, what color *is* your dress?"

I could barely admit it. "Navy blue," I mumbled.

"Oh, that's nothin'," she said, finally looking up, her eyes not smiling even when the corners of her mouth turned up. "We'll just change your line. When you rise up out of the box, you can say, 'And a navy blue dress, too.'" *You mean you can change the words after they're already on the page?*

Elementary school teachers wield a lot of power. And wisdom, too.

Blind Faith

The creek had a dual personality. Mother had expressed her misgivings about it that late afternoon, even before Daddy edged our old Chevy up to it and stopped.

After several hours of a steady downpour, the usually docile creek was now a raging torrent. Unable to contain the surging storm water that cried out for acceptance within its banks, the streambed had hugely overflowed. The one-lane wooden bridge about three car lengths long, now completely inundated by a turbulent muddy flow, was a distant memory. And the rain was still pouring down.

John and I looked at each other in silence, both of us knowing to keep our mouths shut. *Don't ask Daddy a question now; he won't like it.*

Slap, swish, slap, swish. The wipers swiping the windshield, Daddy reached for his handkerchief and wiped the condensation off the inside of the glass, as if by seeing better he could think better.

Slap, swish, slap, swish. "If we're gonna get home today," said Daddy grimly, "we have to go now, before the water gets even higher." Cautiously, he shifted into low gear and slowly inched the car into the swirling murky water.

This simple act was an exercise in blind faith. Faith that the bridge had not been swept downstream in the water. Faith that the bridge would hold up under the weight of the car and the force of the water. Faith that the motor wouldn't stall and leave us stranded in the water. Faith that the wheels wouldn't slip off the edge of the bridge and spill us into the water.

Mother's faith was clearly lacking in at least one of these. "Be careful, Sterlin'," she pleaded anxiously, shifting uneasily in her seat, her forehead pressed against the window as she looked down in a futile effort to see the bridge.

"I *am* bein' careful," snapped Daddy, his usual calm demeanor suffering a stress fracture. Hunched forward, his arms draped across the top of the steering wheel, he stretched his neck in a focused effort to see as far as possible beyond the hood of the car.

John and I peered out the side windows. Had I been wiser, I would have been frightened. But the luxury of ignorance in a hazardous situation is excitement, and I was very excited as we ventured farther into the deluge, the slow grinding whir of the motor a comforting reassurance as the water swirled about the car.

The crossing was quickly over.

"Whew!" a breathless Mother exhaled as we rolled onto muddy ground. "It sure is scary when you look down and all you can see is water!"

"That's why I didn't look down *at* the water," said Daddy. "I looked up at where the road came *out* of the water." Then, tentatively patting her on the knee in an effort to mend his fences, he said what St. Paul said to the early church and what coaches all over the world still say to athletes: "You gotta keep your eye on the goal, ya' know."

Given to arguing, Mother opened her mouth. *Uh-oh! Daddy's gonna be sorry he said that!* But in a surprising change of mind, Mother closed her mouth as silently as she had opened it.

Perhaps she was thinking then what I'm thinking now: Daddy had all sorts of ways to manage fear. He was a coal miner.

The Big City

It was a poor combination: two kids on a long trip and the confined space of a car. The close quarters had done a job on John and me, and Mother had already yelled at us twice.

We were on our way to Evansville to visit Grandma Harris, who had moved there to be near her only living daughter. Aunt Mayfair had survived her older sister, Annabelle, who had died during pregnancy before John and I were born. Now married to an Indiana farmer, Aunt Mayfair lived in a big two-story farmhouse in one of Evansville's outlying German farm communities. Sometimes when we visited Grandma, we also called on Aunt Mayfair and Uncle Herman; we would not do so today because we had something else in mind.

We were less than halfway there, and John and I were already in trouble. This time, it was Daddy who yelled at us. "You kids behave yourselves, or the next time we go to see Grandma Harris, we'll leave you at home." *Huh! You haven't let us stay by ourselves yet!* The highlight of the trip to Evansville was crossing the bridge across the Ohio River, the boundary between Kentucky and Indiana. The sight of the steel span, its roadway suspended on huge cables stretched between soaring towers, never failed to thrill me, and in a time before cars had seatbelts, I sat forward on the edge of my seat to spot the bridge as soon as it rose against the distant horizon. It wasn't just that the graceful overhead structure was beautiful; it was that the bridge itself was so long and so high above the river. I always begged Daddy to slow down on the crossing so it would take longer, and he always did, if the traffic wasn't pushing too close behind us.

The Kentucky side of the upslope to the bridge began back in the rich bottomland of the flat cornfields. *Here we go!* Soon we were in the middle of the bridge and I was looking down. The river was as calm as a millpond, its smooth surface reflecting the trees shading the banks. *Wonder what it would feel like to jump off?*

I had once tied a bath towel around my neck and jumped off the roof of the lean-to that served as the Strongs' soybean bin, absolutely certain that if I concentrated very hard, I would float gently to the ground. *Maybe the reason I didn't float was because the soybean bin wasn't high enough.*

"You'd be dead before you hit the water," said John from the other end of the seat. *How does he know what I'm thinkin'?* It wasn't a real consideration, anyway. For one thing, Daddy would never stop the car on the bridge for me to get out. And for another, I wouldn't get out.

The down slope to Indiana was truly a downer. Almost immediately we were on ground, having crossed the bridge far too quickly for it to have been the focus of the entire trip. *At least we get to go over it again on the trip home.*

139

Evansville was the biggest city I'd ever visited. Down the street from the house where Grandma Harris rented a small room was a street vendor with his cart. "Tuh-mah-*lees*, hot tuh-mah-*lees*," rang out the tenor singsong of the man with the sun-darkened skin, his droopy black mustache hiding his upper lip and the corners of his mouth. "Get your hot tuh-mah-lees *here*-uh!"

"What's a hot tamale, Grandma?"

"Mexican food, meat rolled up in cornmeal and a corn husk."

What's she talkin' about? You can't eat a cornhusk! But when Daddy walked John and me down to the vendor's cart and bought us each a tamale, I understood. *Of course! You don't eat the husk; it's just a wrapper, like paper around a sandwich.*

After we left Grandma's, we went to the zoo. It wasn't much of a zoo, in retrospect—just Big Kay the elephant, a few monkeys and snakes, a few birds and a lion. But it was a treat to go there, especially cracking the shells and picking out the meat of the hot roasted peanuts Daddy bought for us. *If a peanut is a vegetable, how come they call it a nut?*

I wasn't ready to head home. And when we did, I felt a little sad, dreaming all the way. *When I grow up, I'll go to the big city and eat tamales and visit the zoo and buy peanuts and stay as long as I want.*

Little girls have big dreams. And no idea that they will ever dream a bigger one.

Bailing Wire and Duct Tape

Night had fallen. I sat looking out the back window of our parked sedan at the lights of the approaching cars.

Daddy had parked the car that Saturday night next to the curb in front of Mr. Proctor's grocery on the eastern edge of Madisonville.

We often stopped there on the way home to buy the fixings for our favorite Saturday night make-it-yourself supper: sliced sugar cured ham and mayonnaise on white bread, with a small chunk of Longhorn cheese and a canned pineapple slice on the side.

"Yes, you can wait in the car if you want to," Mother had said when I asked. I had few opportunities to be alone, and I liked the grownup way it made me feel, even though the rest of the family would be inside the store for only a few minutes.

Daddy remembers when nobody here had cars and people rode in horse drawn wagons and buggies. Many times he had told the story of the first car he ever saw. A car—one car—had come to Madisonville in 1903, but when its several joint owners couldn't keep it running, they got rid of it. By the time a car came to rural coal country outside of Madisonville, it was 1916. A man had run down the road excitedly knocking on doors and yelling, "Here comes a car, here comes a car!" And by the time it got there, Daddy and his family and all the neighbors had emptied out of their houses and were standing on the side of the road to see the car as it passed.

I liked watching the headlights get bigger and brighter as the oncoming cars neared. *Maybe I'll count how many cars I see. Here comes one now. It's gettin' closer. Wait! It looks like it's gettin' too close. It is too close! Oh, no, it's way too close!*

Crash! Metal against metal. Instantaneous jolt. Arms and legs flopping like Blue Rag Doll, I landed on the other side of the back seat, my head crashing into the post between the front and back doors. I slumped in the corner, temples pounding.

Psychological denial immediately began an internal debate with reason.

What was that?

Nothin'. You imagined it.

No, I didn't. That car sideswiped Daddy's and kept right on goin'.

No, because if it had, Mother and Daddy would have heard it and come runnin' out of the store.

But maybe they didn't hear.

Knees shaking, I slid across the seat, rolled down the window and stuck my head outside. Sure enough, both fenders and doors were scraped and dented, one door handle broken off and tossed aside on the pavement, the other handle dangling crazily at an angle from the door.

Oh, no! It's not my imagination. I struggled a moment, choking back tears. *You're a big girl. Don't cry.*

The jammed back door wouldn't budge. Sliding back across the seat, I opened the other door, fearfully venturing across the sidewalk and into the store to break the news. "What?" cried Mother, bending down to look into my eyes.

"I'm okay," I said. "My head just hurts a little."

"I guess it's from the bouncin' around," Daddy said, running his hands through my hair and over my scalp. "I don't feel any bumps or anything. I think you'll be all right." Then he led the whole family outside to inspect the damage.

No, I didn't know what color the other car was. No, I hadn't seen a license plate. No, I didn't know if the other car had been damaged. No, I didn't know how many people were in the car. No, I hadn't seen the other car; its lights were too bright in my eyes. With nothing to go on, we settled for chattering about the accident all the way home.

No money? No automobile insurance? Car not worth the investment in repairs? No spare parts because the post-war economy was still gearing up? Whatever the reason, Daddy wired the damaged doors shut and drove the car as it was, all of us sliding in on the same side when we went somewhere.

A few weeks later, we all loaded into the car and Daddy backed it out of the garage. Having repeated the process hundreds of times, he had acquired the skill to deftly curve around the tree that stood about two car lengths away in direct line with the center of the garage opening. What masterstroke of planning had allowed our predecessor in Bosses Row to build a garage behind the tree, or to plant a tree in front of the garage doorway, I can't imagine. But this time when Daddy backed the car out, a gross miscalculation preceded a dull thud and a jarring halt.

Jumping out of the car, Daddy inspected the deep crease in the bumper and the dent in the trunk lid. "Well, what do you know!" he exclaimed, scratching his head in amazement. "Somebody moved the tree!"

Don't laugh! John and I clapped our hands over our mouths, not daring to look at each other lest we lose control of our giggles. *This is too serious to laugh, don't laugh!*

Uttering not another word, Daddy quietly got back into the car, backed around the tree and pulled away, all of us silently acquiescing to the pretense that denied us the luxury of accusation and spared him the condemnation of blame.

"We gotta make do," said Mother afterward. "We're savin' our money so we can get a house in Madisonville where the kids can go to better schools." So a few days later, Daddy cut several strips off a roll of duct tape and covered the dent in the trunk lid. "Maybe that'll keep the rust out," he said, standing back and surveying his handiwork. It didn't.

After that, we rode in a rattletrap held together with bailing wire and duct tape. It wasn't an embarrassment; it was a necessity.

And none of us ever mentioned the moveable tree.

Duty Performed

Mother blanched. She gasped, one hand unconsciously fluttering up to her open mouth as if to block whatever else threatened to escape. "Have a seat, Miz Harris," said the miner, quickly sliding a kitchen chair underneath her.

I had not heard the visitor's knock, had not heard him enter the kitchen or his opening words. But I heard him now. "The ambulance has already come for him," he said. *Ambulance? What for?* "You and the kids come with me; I'll drive you to the hospital." *Oh, no! Somethin' bad has happened to Daddy!*

The roof, the overhead structure of rock above the seam of coal in the mine's working area, had caved in on Daddy, the miner said. *You mean the roof can fall?* I had heard Daddy talk about miners leaving pillars of coal in the right places to prevent the roof and the floor from squeezing together under the weight of the earth above, had heard him say that miners set wooden props underneath the roof to provide extra support. *Why didn't the pillars and props work?*

"I don't think he's gonna die," said the man, answering the question he knew Mother was afraid to ask. "He was talkin' when we loaded him in the ambulance. But he's hurt pretty bad, I think."

We rode in silence.

Like a tossed rock skipping off water, my thoughts skipped from the scene in the kitchen to school, to play, and then back to the scene in the kitchen, as if my mind were afraid to settle where it knew it should. But I said nothing, nor did John, neither in the car nor in the hospital reception room where we waited while Mother and the coal-blackened man went upstairs to Daddy's room.

"The Lord was with your daddy today; otherwise, he'd be dead," a tight-lipped Mother said later when she found John and me absentmindedly leafing through the children's books the woman behind the reception desk had handed us. "He'll be in bed a long time this summer, though. The fallin' rock fractured his pelvis, and the doctor says where the break is, it can't be set. Daddy will have to keep his weight off the bone until God knits it back together."

It was a sweltering summer, the heat rising in waves from the sun-baked earth, the unrelenting humidity hanging thickly in the air and plastering our damp clothes to our moist skin. A breeze was a rumor.

The discomfort of the summer was an extra burden for an active man forced to lie in bed, but Daddy's only complaint was that he couldn't go to the mine. As far as I know, he never considered not going back. Coal mining was all he knew, and as risky as it was, it was how he fed his family.

Duty performed casts a rainbow light on the soul, said Theodore Roosevelt. And that's why Daddy's soul is flooded with rainbow light.

The Color of Courage

"Mr. Sterlin', Mr. Sterlin'!" called a deep voice. I peeked out the front window to see a gray-bearded African American man standing in the yard in his mining clothes.

"Yes?" Mother said, opening the screen door and stepping out onto the front porch.

"Howdy, Ma'am." The man removed his hard cap, revealing hair as gray as his beard. "I jes' come to see how Mr. Sterlin's a-doin'."

"Well, he's gettin' pretty impatient bein' laid up and all. He's rarin' to get up and get back to work. C'mon in and say hello to him."

"Oh, no, Ma'am, I can't do that. Jes' tell him I come to see how he's a-doin'."

"No, you c'mon in and tell him yourself." The man hesitated. "It's all right, c'mon in," said Mother, gesturing toward the door.

"Oh, no, Ma'am. I got on my dirty clothes."

"That's okay, we're used to that." He paused, then turned and started around to the back of the house. "No," Mother said to his back, increasing the size of her motions toward the front door. "You come in this way."

He stopped, half turning around. "Oh, no, Ma'am, I can't do that."

"Yes, you can." Mother insisted. "And you will, too, if you care about Sterlin'. Nobody who cares enough to come see about my husband is comin' in my back door!"

No one refused Mother when she used her stern voice. Tentatively the man turned around and approached the porch, tentatively he ascended the steps, tentatively he walked through the door Mother held open for him.

The reluctant visitor refused the kitchen chair Mother placed beside Daddy's bed. Nervously threading the edge of his cap through his fingers, he shifted his weight awkwardly from one leg to the other as Daddy and he made small talk. He didn't stay long.

"Who was that?" I asked after he left.

"Zeke Washin'ton," said Daddy. "He works on my crew. He's a good man, but I think walkin' through that front door took just about all the courage he could get up in one day. Ol' guys like that ain't used to people treatin' 'em right. It's a shame."

We lived in a shabby house at the mouth of a coal mine, and Mr. Washington thought he wasn't good enough to come in our front door? It was a shame, all right, and it was a revelation. One I didn't know what to do with.

First Strike

An eerie sensation crawled up my spine like a spider up a downspout. At the mine, a train was rolling slowly down the track, uniformed soldiers with rifles strapped to their backs standing in open cattle cars and facing the tipple. The miners were on strike; even the air was ominous.

Mother and Daddy had talked about the strike, even before I saw the picture of John L. Lewis in *The Madisonville Messenger*. With his bushy black eyebrows hanging heavily over his eyes, the President of the United Mine Workers of America was unforgettable. By the time the picture appeared, the miners had already formed a picket line in front of the tipple. Parading back and forth with hand-painted signs on their backs, they waved placards in the air and chanted, "No union, no work."

"What are the soldiers doin', Mother?"

"Makin' sure nobody gets killed." *Killed?*

"What do you mean, killed?"

"The miners don't like the scabs and don't want 'em crossin' the picket line, so the governor called out the National Guard to keep the scabs and the miners from fightin' each other." *Scabs?*

"What do you mean, scabs?" I knew she didn't mean the rough crusty patches that formed over a scratch on the skin.

"The men who took the jobs the strikers walked out on. The strikers want their jobs back when the strike is over, and they're afraid the scabs will get the jobs."

It didn't make sense to me. If the strikers wanted the jobs, why did they walk out on them? And how would the strikers get money if they didn't have a job? And how could anybody blame the scabs who took the jobs if they didn't already have one? I knew Mr. Harper and Mr. Burden weren't going to the mine in the mornings now, but Daddy still went every day.

"Is Daddy a scab?"

"No, Daddy's a foreman. He still has to go to the mine every day to check the ventilation and be sure that there's not an explosion or somethin'. Daddy can't belong to the union, so it's okay for him to go to work." *How come they won't let Daddy belong to the union? He's as good as they are!*

147

That night, Mother cornered Daddy. "You're not goin' up in that tipple one more mornin' to raise the flag, not if I have my way," she said, her voice rising. "You're just a sittin' duck up there for anybody who wants to take a shot at you." *Somebody might shoot Daddy?* "Now, Mary, it's my job; I gotta do it," said Daddy calmly. "Anyway, I'll be okay. They all know me and they know I don't have nothin' to do with all this stuff."

It was the first labor strike I had ever seen, and I understood nothing about it. But I was too scared to ask any more questions.

The Kentucky Trinity

Daddy reached for his fiddle and I read the expression on Mother's face. *Here it comes again, the Great Depression story.* I didn't mind; it was often the prelude to a concert.

"Durin' the Depression," Mother began, "your daddy used to walk all the way down the railroad track to Muhlenberg County to play in fiddlin' contests. And he always won." The ball of crochet thread in her lap gradually unwound as her busy hands repeatedly ran the metal hook through a loop and pulled the thread back through, creating a bedspread. How she could talk and not lose track of what she was doing was a mystery to me, but she could.

To know Mother was to know her needlework. At first, it was crocheted doilies, their ruffled edges standing upright under the power of the wet sugar-starch she dipped them into before meticulously ironing them stiff and dry. Later came crocheted tablecloths, knitted afghans, embroidered pillowcases and dishtowels, braided rugs, patchwork and appliquéd quilts, crewel embroidered pictures and throw pillows, a needlepoint cover for the piano stool. She worked while she rested, she said.

"Your daddy would come walkin' back all hunched over," she

continued, "usin' one hand to balance on his back the 50-pound sack of flour he'd won and usin' the other hand to carry his fiddle case." Looking up to be sure that she had my attention, she went on with the crocheting and the story. "I don't know what we would've done if your daddy wasn't a good shot and if he couldn't play the fiddle. Nobody had much of anything then, and the prize was always food."

"Yeah, times were bad," agreed Daddy, his speech clipped as he tuned the fiddle. Gripping it underneath his chin, he drew the bow across the strings with one hand, simultaneously using the other hand to turn the pegs as he spoke through his clenched teeth. "There weren't enough jobs to go around, and lots of people didn't have enough to eat. But we always had somethin' to eat, even if it wasn't fancy. We never went hungry."

"Uh-huh," Mother agreed. "Mr. Proctor always let your daddy buy ammunition on credit, and Daddy never went huntin' that he didn't bring back somethin' for us to eat."

Daddy was the best shot in the family; everybody said so. He had a good eye and a steady aim, they said. "And when we would get some money, even a little bit," Mother said, "we always went to Mr. Proctor and paid somethin' on our account."

"That was before President Roosevelt set up the WPA and I got a job," added Daddy. "The WPA was what saved us."

The U.S. Works Progress Administration was what saved a lot of families during the Great Depression. And that's why a lot of people, even after the Depression was over, displayed pictures of President Franklin Delano Roosevelt and John L. Lewis on the wall right up there beside the picture of Jesus.

It was a familiar sight, a coal miner's homage to the Kentucky trinity.

After the Fall

I was very shaky. Either that or Blue Lightning was.

One hand grasping the seat of my new bicycle, Daddy ran along beside me balancing the bike as I pedaled. "C'mon, c'mon, you can do it," he cheered.

His pelvis had healed, but he had a bit of a limp now and couldn't run as fast as before the accident. Soon I had picked up so much speed that Daddy had to turn loose. I wibble-wobbled forward a few yards and jumped off, falling on my side and ditching the bike.

"Here's how you stop," said Daddy, reaching me just as I scrambled up. Retrieving the bike from the dry shallow ditch, he showed me how to push backward on the pedal and brake the coaster-style bike. A few more tries and I was up and running, if not terribly proficient.

"Let me try yours," I said a few weeks later when John dismounted Red Flyer. I was riding easily and effortlessly now, and getting adventurous.

Gone were the days when I was as tall as John, so his bike was a little taller and heavier than mine. Stretched between the handlebars and the seat was the horizontal cross bar that differentiated a boy's bike from a girl's. Still, I had practiced mounting my bike the way John mounted his, and I could handle his bike, I thought. I anchored my left foot on the left pedal, held the bike by its handlebars and used my right foot to push the bike forward a couple of steps, put all my weight on my left foot and slung my right leg across the rolling bike to the pedal on the other side.

But I was wrong. John's bike wasn't a little taller and heavier than mine; it was a *lot* taller and heavier. Almost as soon as I pedaled out of sight, I took a spill, the crossbar striking me hard between the legs.

Is a boy's pain from a blow to the crotch worse than a girl's? I don't know. I only know that the pain I experienced was like nothing

I had ever known. Even now, I cringe when I think about it. Thankfully, my fall had occurred in private. I lay on the ground groaning and rolling from side to side until I recovered, then pushed John's bike home and said nothing.

The next morning, I was shocked to see an enormous bruise between my legs and trailing down my inner thighs. I could barely walk; even sitting was painful.

"What's the matter with you, Carole Sue?" asked Mother.

"Nothin'."

"Don't tell me nothin'! You're not walkin' like that for no reason."

How does she always know?

I was no match for Mother. Out tumbled the confession, one hand involuntarily reaching toward my crotch. "Let me take a look," she said, "I might have to take you to the doctor." *Look? You mean I have to let you see? You mean I might have to let a doctor see?*

"No, I'll be okay," I resisted, faking self-confidence.

"Don't argue with me, child!" Then, sensing the shyness I had developed about my body, she softened. "I'll look real fast and I promise not to tell anybody."

"Not even Daddy?"

"Not even Daddy."

"And not John, either."

"Okay."

The pain of the injury was nothing compared to the indignity of Mother's examination, as quick and painless as it was. I closed my eyes and pretended it wasn't happening. "I think you'll be all right," said Mother. "You'll just have to take it easy a few days until--"

Until it gets well. I know.

My bruised body healed quickly; my bruised pride took a little longer. And just like Adam and Eve, my real lesson came after the fall: No embarrassment lasts forever.

Good Luck Charm

Daddy and I walked through the field. I felt honored that he had chosen me for this opportunity; quail hunting with Daddy was an activity usually reserved for John.

"You have to be really quiet," Daddy had cautioned before we left the house. "You can't talk once we get out in the field." My lips were sealed tomb tight.

Working the field in front of us, Judy abruptly stopped and raised a front paw, the English Setter's tail sticking straight out, every muscle in her lean body taut as she stood dead still. *The birds are here somewhere, hidin' nearby in the tall grass!*

Judy last year had presented us with puppies. One day, Mother had wadded up some old blankets and made a bed on the floor of the back porch beside the washing machine. "You kids go in the kitchen," she said. "Judy's gettin' ready to have puppies." *Puppies? We're gonna get puppies?*

For the next few hours, Mother periodically went out to the back porch and came back into the kitchen to report to John and me. "She's got another one," she smiled each time. Finally, there were seven puppies.

During the next eight or nine weeks, John and I watched the puppies nurse, start to wobble around, open their eyes and gradually grow bigger until Daddy gave them away, one by one. We hated to see them go, but Judy had a reputation as a good hunter, and plenty of men at the mine were eager to have one of her puppies.

Now several yards behind Judy, Daddy held out his hand and signaled me to stop. "Steady," he said to Judy, raising the shotgun to his shoulder. "Steady." Trained well, Judy recognized the command and held her point; she would break her stance only when Daddy gave her a new command.

Ever so cautiously, Daddy slowly moved forward, prepared each breathless split second for a flash of quail to rush the sky. As loath as Judy was to move a muscle, I stood frozen in my tracks. Except for Daddy's quiet, measured advance, nothing stirred; even the air was still. Then, abruptly, a feathered blur split the air, a small covey of quail on the wing. Pointing his shotgun, Daddy gently squeezed the trigger. Bam! Like rocks from the sky, two birds dropped to the ground.

It was a feat wasted on me, for I lacked the knowledge to appreciate it.

The first part of Judy's job done, now began the second. "Dead bird," said Daddy. At the new command, Judy broke her point and trotted off. Seconds later, yards in front of us, she gently grasped a bird between her teeth and trotted back toward us. Meeting her halfway, Daddy removed the bird from her mouth, stowed the bird in the game pocket of his hunting coat, and reached down to stroke Judy's head.

"Dead bird," said Daddy a second time. Again Judy trotted off, shortly sniffing out the other bird only a few yards beyond the place where the first bird had fallen. "Good girl," said Daddy as we advanced toward her. Removing the bird from her mouth, he stroked her head again and scratched behind her ears. "Good Judy, good girl!" Warming to the praise, she wagged her tail vigorously, her entire body a tightly controlled bundle of energy as she panted her self-satisfaction. Daddy, grinning broadly, stowed the second bird with the first one inside his game pocket.

"I think I'd better bring you with me every time," said Daddy, smiling and patting me on the shoulder. "You're my little good luck charm." *Ooo, I'm Daddy's little good luck charm. Just like the four-leaf clover Mother keeps in the cedar chest!*

I was as proud as Judy was. Oh, I knew I wasn't a good luck charm and that I had done nothing to help Daddy bag two quail with one shot. But now I also knew something else: I was important to Daddy.

153

It was a throwaway comment. In fact, had Daddy been asked, he probably would have said the most significant thing he did that day was bag two birds with one shot.

He would have been wrong.

Say What?

Standing on the school playground, Virginia Mae and I eyed the four big white letters the vandals had painted on the playground's rusty metal trash barrel. "What does it mean?"

"I don't know," said Virginia Mae. "But it's somethin' awful. Otherwise, all the boys wouldn't be snickerin'."

I agreed. When the boys acted like that, it had something to do with things grownups didn't like to talk to kids about. "And Tommy said he and Nancy Jean had done it," volunteered Virginia Mae. Nancy Jean was in our class, and Tommy was in fifth grade.

"Done what?"

"Whatever it means."

"Let's go back in early and ask Miz Larkin before everybody else comes back," I suggested. Miz Larkin didn't mind how many questions we asked, and she had an answer for everything. But if we didn't get back to the room early, we'd never be able to catch our fourth grade teacher alone. Virginia Mae and I both knew without saying that this wasn't a question to ask in front of the whole class.

"Well, I'll tell you," said Miz Larkin, her nose red and raw from a cold that had left her eyes looking sadder than usual. Then she paused. *Uh-oh! This is too long a pause.* "You ask your mothers." Miz Larkin reached for a handkerchief to stifle a sneeze, the simple act a silent dismissal. *Wow, this is really serious.*

Riding home on the bus that afternoon, I dreaded my upcoming chore. *This is gonna be worse than when I asked Mother where babies come from.* Mother had gotten teary eyed when she told me, ending with, "You come to me any time you want to know somethin', and if I don't know the answer, we'll go to a doctor and find out."

Go to a doctor? Ooo-eee! I knew Mother didn't look forward to any more conversations like that, and neither did I.

"Did you ask your Mother?" asked Virginia Mae the next day at recess.

"Uh-huh," I lied, ashamed to admit that I had chickened out.

Now, if "cool" had been a term in the 1940s, Virginia Mae's mother would have been cool. She, according to Miz Bessie, got her long platinum hair out of a bottle. Everything she wore was put together perfectly, shoes and purse matching and both coordinated with her outfit—brightly colored pullover sweaters, wine red lipstick and oversized golden loop earrings almost as big around as bracelets. I had once seen a man in Madisonville follow her with his eyes when she walked by, her high heels clicking on the sidewalk and her hips swaying, swishing her skirt from side to side. "Get your eyes back in your head!" Mother had muttered sharply when Daddy apparently noticed what the other man had noticed. *I bet Virginia Mae wasn't even scared to ask her mother.*

"I did, too," said Virginia Mae. "But Mama said not to worry, Nancy Jean won't have no baby."

"WHAT?"

"Mama said Nancy Jean wouldn't have no baby, 'cause she's too young." Then, noticing my open mouth and surprised wonder, Virginia Mae backed up a step. Folding her arms across her chest, one foot tapping the ground, she confronted me. "Carole Sue," she said skeptically "you didn't even ask your mama, did you? You don't even know what I'm talkin' about, do you?"

No, but by the end of recess, I did.

Seven. Rainbow Broken

They have broken your heart, I know,
and the rainbow gleams of your youthful
dreams . . .[7]

                      – James Whitcomb Riley

A Real Bad Run

My mind was made up; I was leaving home. I was having a bad run with Mother and Miz Baxter, my fifth grade teacher, and I just couldn't take it anymore.

At school, I couldn't be quiet when I was supposed to and I was getting C's in Deportment. Both Miz Baxter and Mother were unhappy. And in our house, when Mother wasn't happy, nobody was happy.

I got A's in everything but Deportment, except when I didn't care and got B's. And I got A's every time, if I worked at it. But even working at it, I couldn't get an A in Deportment, couldn't even get a B. I knew what Miz Baxter expected of me, but often I forgot and spoke out without permission. "Miz Baxter says Carole Sue gets her work done so fast that she gets bored," Mother had told Daddy.

If not a compliment, it was at least a partial explanation. But it was little consolation, for at home, I seemed to be in trouble all the time. For what, I don't remember; I just remember how miserable I was.

One day, in a fit of desperation, I sat down on the back porch steps to plan my getaway. *Mother hates me. She'd rather have the baby who died than have me. She always says, 'You lived,' like 'You lived and he didn't,' like it was my fault. She likes boys better than girls, and I know it because she's not as mean to John as she is to me. And Daddy doesn't even seem to notice.*

My self-commiseration darkened, the story of the little yellow house having temporarily disappeared from my radar screen. *In fact, I bet I'm not even theirs. I don't even look like Mother, or Daddy, either. Her face is round and mine is square. Daddy's*

159

nose curves up in the middle and my nose is straight. I bet somebody left me on the doorstep and they thought they had to take me. I'll just run away. They don't want me, anyhow. No, wait—I have a better idea. I'll pretend I'm dead. And when they start to cry, I'll jump up and say, 'Ha! I'm not even dead.' And I'll laugh when they get all mad because I fooled 'em.

Then I remembered Mark Twain's Tom Sawyer. When he lay down and pretended he was dead to make people sorry for mistreating him, they not only weren't sorry, they even dumped a pitcher of water on him to make him get up. *Mother and Daddy probably would do somethin' like that to me, too. And if I ran away, they wouldn't even miss me, much less be sorry. It wouldn't do any good to run away if they weren't sorry.*

I ruled it out. Not because Mother and Daddy wouldn't miss me, but because it wouldn't work. Where would I go? I had no way to get to anyone who would take me in. And if I did, Mother would find out, like she always found out everything, and then I would be in worse trouble than I was already in. If I thought I was having a bad run now, running away would be a *real* bad run—bad enough to find out what Mother meant by *real* trouble.

One day, Mother left the kitchen radio on while I was having a bath. "Is your life goin' wrong? Are you unhappy? Jesus can change all that," declared a radio preacher. "You can be saved right now, right this very instant! All you have to do is just touch the radio and accept Jesus while I pray this prayer of forgiveness. Wherever you are, whatever you're doin', just reach out and touch the radio. Don't be shy. Jesus will save you and turn your life around."

That's exactly what I need. If I was saved, I'd be good and Mother wouldn't have to get mad at me, and Miz Baxter wouldn't give me C's in Deportment. I was out of the tub and headed for the radio before I remembered. *Daddy says never to touch anything electric when you're wet.* Quickly drying my hands, I put one on the radio and closed my eyes as the preacher prayed.

Nothing happened.

I waited.

Still, nothing happened. Opening my eyes, I examined my hands, looked at my face in the mirror hanging over the washstand. *Right, nothin's happened.* The preacher still praying, I put my hand back on the radio, closed my eyes again and waited some more.

Nothing happened.

I opened my eyes again. *Somethin's wrong here. That dumb ol' preacher can't even make it work! What good is he?*

I got back into the tub and made my plan. *Well, at least not everybody hates me. My friends seem to think I'm okay, and Miz Baxter, too, except for the deportment part. Mother does, too, mostly. I'll just not worry so much about what she thinks. And when I'm grown, it won't matter anyhow.*

I had resorted to a child's last refuge: believing that all my problems would go away when I was grown.

Rudder of Imagination

I blamed the preacher, not the radio. The radio was too good to be blamed for anything, much less a preacher who couldn't get somebody saved.

How the radio worked, I had no idea. I didn't even care. I didn't know how electricity worked, either, or how the stars hung up in the sky, or where coal came from. God made it all, according to Mother. But God wasn't making any more coal, Daddy had said—He's already made all He wants. There were so many mysteries in the world, it just didn't make sense to worry about where things came from or how they worked. "Just enjoy it," said Mother. "If God didn't make it directly, He taught somebody how to. So—"

So I enjoyed radio. There was *The Grand Ole Opry* on Saturday nights. "How-dee!" called Minnie Pearl in her trademark opening. "I'm jes' so proud to be here!"

And there was *Stella Dallas*, the soap opera we listened to on weekday afternoons in the summer when Grandma Harris came to visit. "That silly Lolly," Grandma said about Stella's daughter, just as if she were a next door neighbor. "She's gonna be the death of Stella yet!"

Oh, yes—and *The Shadow*. "Who knows what evil lurks in the heart of man?" a deep male voice intoned, hooking the listener before laughing darkly, "Ha Haaaa! The Shadow knows!"

News about important world events was on the radio, too. When Israel became a nation, the radio carried the news. Why I remember it, I have no idea, except that the local radio preachers made a big deal out of it, linking it to biblical prophecy.

And when I heard on the radio that Princess Elizabeth, the heir to the throne of England, had married Prince Phillip in much pomp and pageantry, I went scurrying to *The Madisonville Messenger* to find a picture of the princess. What could more captivate a young girl's fantasy than a real fairy tale wedding of a real princess, a real horse-drawn carriage pulled through the streets of London to the cries of cheering throngs of people, a real wedding gown with yards and yards of beautiful white lace and a train so long that little girls carried it, a real jeweled crown, and a real prince to carry the princess away to a real palace?

Radio wasn't like movies; movies presented a make-believe world. But the radio, alongside its make-believe world, also presented a real world with real people and real events.

I loved radio. It was the rudder of my imagination.

Smoky Mouth of Danger

A huge plume of black smoke billowed up on the horizon. "Where's it comin' from?" wondered Mother, anxiously surveying the sky outside the car window as we drove home from Madisonville that Christmas Eve. I was eager to get home to Daddy's birthday cake. "It don't look like wood smoke; it's too black," said Daddy. "It's comin' from the direction of East Diamond."

We regularly passed East Diamond mine on our drive to and from Madisonville. With the longest continuous conveyer belt in the world, the mine had opened to the talk of the entire state. Gone were the mules and gone were the vertical shaft and cage. The miners walked down a sloped incline to their work at the seam of coal, where motorized Joy loaders and shuttle cars handled the excavated coal before dumping it onto the looped conveyer belt of reinforced rubber for carrying up the slope to the tipple. After the miners finished their shift, they simply sat down on the belt and rode up, sliding off onto the ground when they reached the mouth of the mine. There was even an industrial washer for the excavated coal. Coal free of unwanted dust and debris—what an innovation!

"Oh, mercy, what if it *is* East Diamond?" worried Mother.

Soon, approaching the mine on our right, we confirmed the worst fear of every miner and his family. The mine was on fire, roiling, churning acrid smoke now pouring out from underground and abnormally darkening the daytime sky. "Goodness gracious! It's gonna be a sad Christmas for somebody, I'm afraid," lamented a cheerless Mother. "Maybe lots of somebodies. Um, um, um!"

How is a fire in a coal mine extinguished? With a continuous supply of fuel, the fire will burn for years until all the coal is consumed. The solution is to erect barriers of concrete block inside the mine, walling off the burning area and starving it of the oxygen needed to keep burning. But first, each miner must be accounted for and either rescued or his body recovered.

Daddy turned the car into the mine's access road and stopped a hundred yards or so away from the tipple. *What's Daddy doin'? He's gonna make us late for his birthday cake!* "I'll be back as soon as I can," he said, cutting off the engine and leaping out of the car all in one motion. Almost certainly, he was aware of the 1925 explosion that killed five miners at Finley Mine in Hopkins County. Nevertheless, off he jogged, his back growing smaller in the distance until he disappeared into the dreadful smoke that now rendered invisible the tipple and all its surrounding outbuildings.

The silence shouted, my pulse pounding my ears. Finally, the frightful question asked itself. "He won't go inside, will he?"

"He'll offer to if it'll help," Mother frowned. "Your daddy's had special trainin' in first aid and mine rescue operations." *Oh.*

"But how can they go inside with all that smoke?"

"I don't know. Maybe they can go down the airshaft instead of down the slope." *There's an airshaft?*

"But Daddy doesn't have his hard cap and headlamp. How can he see?"

"Maybe they have spares he can borrow." *Oh.*

"But it's not Daddy's mine. Don't they have their own rescuers?"

Long pause. "If your daddy was trapped inside when the mine caught on fire, you wouldn't care who went in to get him out, would you?"

She was right and I knew it. All my arguments exhausted, I gave up. Long minutes passed, much more than an hour, it seemed, before we saw Daddy walking back toward the car. "Here he comes," said Mother, visibly relaxing.

Because of the holiday, Daddy told us, only a few men were inside. The rescue work was already underway; Daddy hadn't gone inside and wouldn't need to.

Decades later, a man would come to Daddy's funeral with a story that Daddy had never told. "Once when Pond River flooded, the backwater headed for the air shaft, threatenin' to flood the mine. So they ordered us to evacuate. But Sterlin' knew I was back in the old works and hadn't heard the order, so he came back in to get me. 'Get outta here,' he yelled, 'we're about to get flooded!' And we ran! The water stopped risin' before it reached the shaft, but he didn't know that was gonna happen. He risked his life to save mine. That's what I call a hero." It was an unsolicited testimony about a man who had proved Samuel L. Clemens' maxim: Courage is the mastery of fear, not the absence of fear.

"Damage Heavy as Fire Hits East Diamond," screamed the headline of *The Madisonville Messenger* the day after Christmas. The caption below the picture of the tipple enshrouded in smoke told the tale: one death and hundreds of thousands of dollars in lost wages, property and operating time.

East Diamond eventually reopened for operation. But on the day of the fire, the day Daddy turned his back to us and walked toward the smoky mouth of danger, I hadn't said, "'Bye, Daddy."

I had been afraid to say it.

Making Music

The fifth grade was mostly boring, except for the music class. "Beep," went the metallic tone of Miz Baxter's shiny round pitch pipe, and the whole class matched the tone. "Loo." Then the tiny sway-backed woman with the clear, bell-like voice sang a line of music from our book. The next time, we sang the line with her. Repeating the process, each time adding another line, we eventually learned the entire song.

I was the only kid in the fifth grade who could already read music, thanks to the private piano lessons Daddy had arranged for me. He had learned from Mr. Lang, the accountant who handed out the paychecks every Saturday at the mine's company store, that his daughter taught piano lessons at their house in Madisonville. Each Tuesday and Thursday after Daddy finished his bath, the whole family rode into town and went to visit one of Daddy's brothers while I went for a piano lesson.

Miss Lang sat in a chair to the right of the piano bench, peering through thick-lensed glasses and tapping her red lead pencil on the music rack as I played. Occasionally stopping me to write a note on the music about something I needed to give particular attention, she used the opportunity to take a sip of coffee from the ever-present cup resting on a small table beside the piano. Miss Lang didn't smile much, but she was frequent with her praise and gentle with her corrections. She seemed to have just the right amount of patience needed to push me a little but not too much as I learned the key signatures, the names of the notes and how to count the timing, where to find them on the piano and which fingers to use to play the notes.

Now at school, Miz Baxter made use of my newly acquired knowledge and let me help with the music class, rotating me from row to row to help the other kids learn the notes. Treble clef, five lines and four spaces. Lines from the bottom up, E, G, B, D, F: **E**very **G**ood **B**oy **D**oes **F**ine; spaces from the bottom up, spell **FACE**.

Oh, how we made music! We sang patriotic songs: "God Bless America;" folk songs: "Oh, Susanna, Don't You Cry For Me;" and the song that still precedes the running of the Kentucky Derby in Louisville, "My Old Kentucky Home." And we did all of this without benefit of a piano or any other accompaniment, an accomplishment that now seems quite remarkable.

The more experience I gained, the more amazed I became that Daddy could play piano and fiddle without reading music. It wasn't long before I knew that he had more natural talent in one finger than

I had in ten. And by the time John began to study violin, we both knew that Daddy had more talent than John and I put together. Still, we worked at it, both of us confronting the agonizing near-paralysis of stage fright during our required recitals and competitions.

And now I know. It was a small price to pay for a love of music that would bring us a lifetime of pleasure.

A Carole is a Carol

"Mother, how do you spell my name?"

She stopped whistling. "What do you mean? You know how to spell your name, don't you?" she said, pouring water into a dishpan.

I was scraping out the supper dishes and stacking them in preparation for the nightly routine of washing and drying them for use again the next morning at breakfast. *I hate it when she answers a question with a question.* "Yes, but I mean, how do *you* spell it? My first name, I mean."

"C-a-r-o-l-e. Why?" Splash, dishes sinking into the soapy water.

"Well, the last time we looked in the cedar chest, I noticed that my birth certificate had 'C-a-r-o-l' on it, but I didn't think to ask you about it at the time."

"Oh, that," said Mother casually. "That's a mistake. I was thinkin' about Carole Lombard at the time I told Dr. Davis to spell your name with an 'e' on the end. Carole Lombard was real pretty, a movie star. Clark Gable's wife, ya' know?" No, I didn't know.

"She got killed later in an airplane crash. Well, anyway, when your birth certificate came out, it didn't have the 'e' on the end of 'Carol.' And when I saw it, I thought it was okay that way. Kinda musical, ya' know?" *Oh, you mean like a Christmas carol?*

"But I noticed in some of my little kid books that you saved, you sometimes wrote my name with an 'e' on the end and sometimes without. And in one book, you wrote it one way on one page and the other way on the opposite page."

"Really? Well, I guess I forget sometimes." *I bet if I was your real daughter, you wouldn't forget!*

The confusion about my name would continue at school and elsewhere, the spelling appearing first one way and then another on school report cards, printed programs and official documents. I eventually opted for the "e," primarily because I had a classmate whose name was Carol without the "e," and I thought the different spelling might differentiate between us. It didn't.

It's okay. A Carole is a Carol. It's a song, no matter how it's spelled.

Sins of the Father

The school bus was crowded. I spotted him in the aisle that afternoon as soon as I boarded. *Ooo, there's Eddie. He's cute! I'm gonna go stand next to him.*

Eddie's parents and he had moved into a new concrete block house recently built in the community, and Eddie had been in my class now for three whole days. *Oh, look—he's taller than I am!* This was a treat, since I was taller than all the other boys in my class and very much wanted not to be.

It was a routine ride until the bus lurched and I lost my footing, bumping into Eddie. Totally without warning, he balled his hand into a fist and slugged me squarely on the upper arm. I staggered from the blow, grabbing the handgrip on the back of the nearby seat to keep from falling. "Watch out what you're doin'," he roared, hostility seeping from his very pores. *Here I am likin' you, and you're nothin' but a bully!*

"What's the matter with you?" I complained, massaging the rising lump on my arm. "It was just an accident."

"Just don't let it happen again!" he threatened, his fist still drawn back. *This is not Bobby Joe, and I haven't got a stick in my hand this time.*

Suddenly, from out of nowhere, I remembered one of Rev. Brown's sermons. "Sinners, beware! Someday the wrath of God is gonna come straight down on top of your head." Willing the tears not to form in my eyes, I took a slight step toward Eddie. It wasn't a plan, it wasn't a scheme, it was nothing like that. "Let me tell you somethin', Eddie Wells," I scowled, pressing an index finger into the center of his chest. "You *ever* touch me again and I'm gonna call the wrath of God straight down on top of your head!"

Confusion flashed across Eddie's eyes. For a moment, toe to toe, we glared at each other. Then he gulped, lowered his fist, turned a shoulder toward me and looked away. "Girls," he muttered.

He said it like a cuss word.

A few days later, driving home from Madisonville, our family passed by Eddie's house. "George says that new guy beats his wife," Daddy told Mother, nodding toward the house. "George said the other day he was drivin' by here when the wife came stumblin' out the door and fell down on the porch. She didn't get up, so George stopped his car and ran up to the porch to see if she needed help. That's when Whatsizname, her husband, came to the door and yelled, 'Don't you dare touch her. She's *my* wife, and nobody touches her but me.'" *No wonder Eddie hit me.*

I had never seen or even heard of domestic violence, but I knew that what was going on in Eddie's family was wrong. And I knew that Eddie had hit me because he had learned from his father that it was acceptable for a man to hit a woman.

It's just as the Bible says. The sins of the fathers extend to the generations.

A Coal Night

Before nightfall, John was supposed to bring coal inside to fire up the heater the next morning. My job was to help John, and Daddy's job was to start the fire. "Everybody's got a job to do," said Daddy. "This is y'all's job."

It usually wasn't a problem. But somehow, something had happened to John's and my resolve to get our work done early, and we had procrastinated. That night when Daddy shoveled up the ashes to dump them on the fire, banking it down at bedtime, he spied the two empty coalscuttles on the hearth.

"What's the coal buckets doin' empty, John Morgan?" It wasn't a question meant to be answered; in fact, Daddy didn't even pause. "Get your coat on and go out to the coalhouse and bring in the coal, like you were supposed to."

"But it's dark. I can't see," whined John, searching for an excuse. *Daddy will feel sorry for him and go get the coal.*

"Yes, you can," said Daddy, "because Carole Sue's gonna hold a light for you. Sis, go get your coat and the flashlight and go to the coalhouse with John."

Two little kids in the shivering cold winter, one shoveling coal and the other holding a flashlight to fend off the night. Shades of Charles Dickens! The coalhouse was barely more than a shack, and it did little to cut the wind that blew across the flat landscape, chilling us to the bone. And since it took both of us to carry a full scuttle of heavy coal, we had to make two trips.

It was a coal night in Kentucky. One more thing to add to my bad run.

Picture This

Mother opened the cedar chest and took out the picture album. "Let's look at pictures today," she said. *Oh, goodie, the picture album.* We spent the whole afternoon with the album, and not a single cross word occurred between us.

Great-Grandma Sisk in a long black dress, her dark hair piled on top of her head. *She looks really grim!*

Grandma and Grandpa Sisk on their wedding day. *Why do the people in old pictures always look so glum?*

A picture of Mother and Daddy on their wedding day. *Daddy was almost completely bald, even when he was only 24. And Mother looked so very young.*

Pictures of John and me as babies. *They sure did make lots of pictures of us.*

A picture of John, Betty Sue, and me standing on the front porch, Judy lying on the floor at our feet. *Look how dark their hair is and how light mine is.*

Mother's four brothers, arms linked across each other's shoulders for the camera. *Mother says it's the only known picture of all of them together.*

Grandpa Sisk when he was 17. *Look at Granddaddy when he was young. See the shape of his nose and his face? That's who I look like, except that I've got Daddy's blue eyes and light hair and skin! I guess I must be Mother and Daddy's kid, after all.*

Millions of dollars are spent every year on family photography, and all for the same reason: people who have photos never have to say goodbye. Proving family lineage is a side advantage for kids having a bad run.

Morning Lament

Wiping the sleep from my eyes, I wandered into the living room where Grandma Harris had slept on our sofa the night before.

Grandma lived out of a suitcase. "Ain't nobody there," she had said about her room and shared bath in the boarding house in Evansville. "Why should I be?" With five living sons and several older grandchildren out on their own, Grandma kept the Greyhound bus company in business as she traveled from family to family, spending two or three weeks at each place before moving on. Unafraid to travel alone but wary that a bus station predator might snatch her purse, she guarded her cash by stowing the bills in her shoes. As for managing her bags, with so little money that she couldn't afford to pay a porter, she depended on the kindness of strangers. "There's always a nice young man around," she would say. Her system worked; she never lost her purse to a snatcher and she received more offers of help with her bags than she could use.

No one would have guessed that the year she would turn 80, determined to visit Uncle Lionel and Aunt Martha on the west coast, Grandma would travel from Evansville to Burbank, California. On the return trip as she changed buses in Nashville, she would take her ticket to an agent and change her destination from Evansville to Miami. Why should she go home to a cold, lonely room when she could visit Uncle Vernon and Aunt Mildred at their winter place in sunny Florida? Coast to coast at age 80! "When I got to Nashville," she would explain to those who marveled at her stamina, "I felt so good that I just couldn't stop."

This time, she had stopped at our place. Now poised on the edge of our sofa, she had adopted her usual position on rising in the morning. It was a position I knew well. Hunched over, elbows resting on her knees and head in her hands, she pulled a little lower over her brow the brightly flowered scarf she called her head rag.

Her only ever-present accessory, it served to cover her nearly bald head. *I guess the Harris men get their baldness from Grandma.*

Resting her chin in her upturned palms, Grandma looked down at the floor. "Oh, me!" she groaned. "Don't nobody care nothin' about me no how." *If I had a nickel for every time I've heard her say that, I'd be rich!* It was her unique phrase, one voiced every morning like a mantra.

"Grandma, why do you always say that? You shouldn't talk like that."

She neither looked at me nor turned in my direction. "Oh, me!" she groaned again. "Don't nobody care nothin' about me no how."

Had I been a little older, I would have known that Grandma was begging the answer. Had I been a little wiser, I would have known to say, "No, Grandma, that's not true. We all love you." But I no more knew what she wanted to hear than she knew how to ask for it.

Daddy's mother had outlived her husband, and in a cruel twist of life that no parent ever expects, had even outlived three of her children. Few experiences are harder than burying an offspring; yet, except for her standard morning lament, she never complained. She didn't deny her troubles, but she gave them only two minutes a day. If that wasn't enough, too bad; she moved on.

If Grandma had stayed in one place long enough, she could have given lessons on how to survive a bad run. But then, perhaps her life was her lesson.

Signs of the Times

We had been on the Greyhound bus forever, Mother, John and I. It was a long way to South Carolina, and we weren't even to Nashville yet.

Uncle Mason had returned from the war with a bride, a shy young woman with a Southern accent, and Betty Sue had gone to live with her daddy and her new mama. After Levry was born, they all moved to South Carolina to be near Aunt Ruth's family, and now baby Gloria had joined Betty Sue and Levry. I was excited about my new cousin and about having Betty Sue to play with again, even if it would be for only a week this time.

"I wish we didn't have to change buses," said Mother.

Kids can always tell when a parent is scared. Mother had never before ridden a bus, had never before gone anywhere without Daddy, except to a neighbor's house. If Mother was scared to change busses, so was I. But when we pulled into the Nashville station, scared or not, we got off to find our connection.

The station was huge. Hoards of people milled about as the public address system reverberated throughout the high-ceilinged terminal, a male voice periodically announcing what bus was on what track and what time the busses would depart. *I can't understand what he's sayin'. How will we know which bus to get on? What if we get on the wrong bus and end up in the wrong place?* But courage mounts with opportunity, and somehow, Mother managed to get us on the right bus.

Soon we were on our way again and I was watching for Burma Shave signs. A planned sequence of five small signs placed near the highway a few hundred feet apart, each sign revealed a single line of rhyming advertisement.

> Hen don't cluck
> Like she useter
> Perhaps she's seen
> A smoother rooster
> Burma Shave

I loved the signs; they made travel interesting.

Car went past
Sure was whizzin'
Fault was her'n
Funeral his'n
Burma Shave

We had crossed the border into South Carolina when I saw the billboard at the edge of an approaching town: "Ku Klux Klan Picnic—Town Park—Music—Food for All—Balloons for the Kids." *What?* I was shocked. I knew about the Ku Klux Klan from a movie I'd seen, and the Klan did awful things to African Americans. The Klanners hid under long white robes and wore hoods over their faces, didn't they, because they were ashamed of the things they did? Weren't they afraid for the police to know who they were?

"You mean they come right out in public without their hoods on, and actually give picnics and stuff, and the police don't put 'em in jail?"

"Honey, you're in the South now," said Mother.

Sometimes Mother gave answers that didn't seem like answers.

Fragile World

John and I awoke at about the same time, the moonlight streaming through our window faintly lighting the room. Sitting up in our beds, we locked eyes in disbelief. Mother and Daddy were arguing. They had argued before, but never like this. This time, the argument was so loud that it had awakened us from a sound sleep.

"You just dare! You come drivin' up in a new car and I'm walkin'

175

out and takin' the kids with me," shouted Mother, tears in her voice. *Oh, no! This can't be happenin'!* It had never occurred to me that Mother and Daddy wouldn't be together always; it simply wasn't in my frame of reference. They thought divorce was a terrible thing; I knew it because of the way they talked about Mr. Larkin leaving Miz Larkin and their kids. If Mother and Daddy split up, what would happen to John and me? *Mother threatened to take us with her, but Daddy would never allow that. What if they ask us to choose?*

John and I sat in the dark, the world as we knew it eroding in the acid drip of the voices in the other room. In hushed whispers, we decided. Mother would be afraid to live alone, so John would go with her; she would need protection. Daddy couldn't cook, so I would go with him; he would need someone to make the sandwiches he took to the mine for lunch every day.

"We'll get the house *after* we get the car," yelled Daddy. "Our ol' rattletrap's fallin' apart. I don't know how much longer I can keep piecin' it back together with bailin' wire and duct tape."

"Let it fall apart, then, see if I care! We've walked before; we can walk again. What do you think we've been scrimpin' and savin' for? No new clothes, no new nothin' forever—doin' without and makin' do the best way we can. So we can move to Madisonville, that's why! We're gonna get a house in town before we get one more thing! John'll be in junior high next year, and he needs to start gettin' ready for high school. A diploma from Anton's not worth the paper it's written on. I don't care what anybody says, car or no car. My kids are *not* gonna graduate from an unaccredited high school!"

The next morning the air was thick with silence, no rainbow gleams, no youthful dreams. I ventured into the unknown with a broken heart and an abundance of caution, lest the slightest sound shatter my fragile world.

Eight. Rainbow Changing

. . . *the changing rainbow of our living relationships*. . .[8]

— D.H. Lawrence

And the Winner Is . . .

The house at 511 Murphy Avenue was so close to the accredited Madisonville High and Junior High School that we could see it from our front porch. "The kids can come home for lunch and they can stay for after-school activities if they want to," smiled Mother.

Whether Mother would have acted on her threat or not, I don't know, but Daddy hadn't put her to the test. He pieced our old rattletrap together one more time and bought the small white asbestos-shingled house. Though it had more rooms than the house at the mine, it was debatable whether it had more room. The separate dining room was a necessity because the kitchen was too small to accommodate a table and chairs. The two bedrooms were odd sizes, the one in front big but the adjoining one in back barely big enough to accommodate a twin bed and still leave walk space beside it to get to the adjacent bathroom.

Bathroom? Yes, bathroom! We now had indoor hot and cold running water and just as miraculously, a natural gas kitchen range and floor furnace. Finally, we would be warm in winter, we wouldn't have to carry coal and we wouldn't have to go outside to the toilet or carry water from a well.

Oh, and yes—there was a telephone. The black instrument miraculously contained a cheery female voice. "Number, please," chirped the nameless, faceless voice when one of us picked up the receiver. After the caller spoke the desired telephone number, just like magic, the operator made the connection. We would soon make friends with people who had phones, and would find it hard to

179

believe that we had ever gotten along without the miraculous communication device.

With these truly wonderful advances, it seemed wrong to complain, but the sleeping accommodations were woefully inadequate, and I knew it immediately. Either John or I would have to sleep in Mother and Daddy's bedroom. How the decision was made I have no idea, but my bed was placed in the small bedroom where I received all the bathroom traffic, and John's bed was placed in Mother and Daddy's bedroom. A bedroom for John would be added to the back of the house later, but for now, the front bedroom was shared space. The house was close to an accredited high school; that was what mattered.

Mother had won the battle, but Daddy hadn't lost. It was a victory for the whole family, a victory that would change our lives forever.

Friends for Life

Stretched across South Main Street at the entry to town was a tall rainbow-arched sign comprised of huge white letters on a field of black: "Madisonville," it read. Underneath it, a straight baseline of smaller letters read, "Welcome to the Best Town on Earth."

I knew it was true when I discovered the public library.

Every afternoon that Mother gave permission, I rode Blue Lightning several blocks to the red brick building on Union Street, walked down the steps to the children's room in the basement, chose a book from the shelf and sat down at one of the tables to read. When it was time to go, I put the book back on the shelf, mentally noting the page number where I had stopped and the location on the shelf where I placed the book. The next time I came back, I would find the book and resume reading where I had stopped.

"You know, you can borrow books to take home and read, if you

180

want to," said the librarian now standing in front of my table. I hadn't heard her approach. *Is that grown woman talkin' to me?* "Really?" I looked up, unconvinced. "Yes, if you promise to return 'em by the date I stamp in the back." "That's all? You mean I don't have to pay?" "Not unless you keep the book past the deadline, and then it's just a penny for each day it's late." *If it's more expensive to live in town than in the country, how come the books are free?*

Mother had taught John and me almost to revere books. She wouldn't let us mark in them, except to write our names on the inside front page. She had even taught us how to open a new book. We opened a few pages in the front and a few pages in the back, used our fingers to press down the indentation at the spine, and repeated the process several times with a few more pages each time until we gradually worked our way to the center. "That way, it won't break the spine," said Mother. "A book is a friend for life, so take care of your books. Read and you'll never be lonely."

I began to check out books, loading the wire basket on Blue Lightning's handlebars with the maximum number of books allowed. The Nancy Drew mystery series. The Bobbsey Twin series. I especially enjoyed a set of biographies with orange covers. George Washington. Abraham Lincoln. Florence Nightingale. George Washington Carver. Abigail Adams. Benjamin Franklin. Thomas Jefferson. Clara Barton. Sometimes I even sat in the front porch swing and read aloud to myself just to hear the sound of the words in my ears, especially in very descriptive passages and in long sections of dialogue. It was faster to read silently, of course, but sometimes not as satisfying.

"Do you know about the books upstairs?" asked the librarian one day.

"What books upstairs?"

"Books for grown people," she said. "We have a lot more books up there than down here. I think you've just about worked the children's section. Let me show you. You might not be interested in everything, but I think you can find somethin' you'll like."

Leading me upstairs, she walked me through the stacks, showing me how to find the various sections: history, fiction, reference, poetry. I was flabbergasted! The library had more books than I had ever dreamed of. "Why don't you try these?" she said, handing me a book of poetry and a biography. "You told me you like to read aloud; you might like poetry. And this book about Clara Barton will tell you a lot more about her than the book you just finished. C'mon on over here with me and fill in a membership card."

The librarian was right. From the book she handed me, I learned more about the founder of the American Red Cross than I had learned from the children's book. And the poetry—what a discovery! It was so much more complex—not all of it rhymed— and so much more descriptive, colorful and filled with emotion than the poems in my school textbooks. I read the poems slowly, allowing them to sink into my mind even when I didn't understand the meaning, enjoying the beauty of the expression and the rhythm of the words, even their very placement on the page. *Imagine! Just to be able to think like that!*

My first summer in Madisonville I knew no one, but I was never lonely. For I had made friends with books, my friends for life.

New Girl

Squeak! *Oh, no, a squeaky door.*

All eyes turned in my direction and followed as I closed the door behind me and edged along the aisle beside the blackboard. I was late, having wandered the halls of Seminary Elementary School until I found a custodian who gave me directions to the sixth grade room.

The two-story red brick building had once housed the high school, but the growing town had built a bigger high school—the one that we could see at the end of the street where we now lived—and had converted Seminary to an elementary school. The wide halls, their black-tiled floors buffed to a high shine, were lined with olive drab metal lockers eventually assigned to individual students. The building itself, much bigger and more imposing than the building at Anton, was enough to intimidate me, even if I had known all the students and teachers.

I had walked to school alone, having learned the route that summer by walking there twice weekly for piano lessons from my new teacher, whose studio was in one of the basement rooms. She taught violin as well as piano, and now that John was studying violin, family logistics were easier if John and I went to our lessons together. So I had switched teachers.

If mothers were supposed to accompany their children on their first day in a new school, Mother didn't know that, and I had no expectation of it. And in a mistake of judgment, I had allowed no extra time to search for my classroom.

Wonder what they do to you at this school when you're late? I had never been counted late to school, because if a bus student arrives late, it's the bus's fault, not the student's. *Next year, all I'll have to do is walk one block to Junior High.* But it wasn't next year yet, and all the wishing in the world wouldn't make this humiliating moment go away.

Summoning all my courage, I crossed the room in front of 25 pairs of eyes, not counting the teacher's, and walked up to her desk. "My name's Carole Sue Harris. I'm comin' from Anton, and my fifth grade teacher told me to give you this." Then I handed her the manila envelope Miz Baxter had given me on the last day of school.

"I'm not supposed to give you this," Miz Baxter had said, "but since you're leavin', I think I have a good reason. Take it to your sixth grade teacher." That day, riding home on the bus, I had opened the unsealed envelope and read the results of the standardized test I had taken a few weeks before school was out. "English Proficiency— 9.5 Grade Level. Math Proficiency—7 Grade Level." I was astounded. Not with my proficiency level, but that my proficiency level had been measured. *Why do they care about that? They're not gonna put me up in the seventh grade just because I can solve seventh-grade math problems. So what difference does it make? And anyway, why does the teacher care? She already knows our grades; she's the one who gives 'em to us, for goodness sake!*

"I'm Mrs. Graham," said the round-faced, rosy-cheeked teacher with the short dark hair. She was sitting down, but even so, I could see that she was tall, her shoulders wide and her hands large. *Missus, not Miz. They talk different in town. I'll have to remember that.* With great relief I slid into the seat she pointed out to me, happy to be no longer the center of attention.

"I knew Carole Sue was a leader the very first time I saw her," Mrs. Graham told Mother at the first parent-teacher meeting, which met after school dismissed for the day. Standing beside mother, I had stayed to walk home with her. "I could tell by the way she marched right up to my desk and introduced herself." *A leader? Kids can be leaders?*

The term came with expectations—of what, I had no idea. And that was the problem. "I'm scared," I told Mother as we walked home, my stomach churning.

"Scared of what?"

"I don't know. Everything's so new and all, and different."

"That's okay," said Mother. "It doesn't mean you're not up to it. It just means you care." *Is that what it means? So maybe it's a good thing?*

Mother had made the move to Madisonville with all the excitement that comes with hope fulfilled, but I had made the move with all the apprehension that comes with change.

And like it or not, I was the new girl—a case study in change.

A Fledgling Faith

Daddy was working at a different mine now, and working graveyard: eleven o'clock at night until seven o'clock in the morning. It was a horrendous grind.

How the graveyard shift got its name, I have no idea. Perhaps it is because nobody is up at that hour except ghosts. Or perhaps it is because most people who work the brutal hours of graveyard adjust poorly to sleeping in the daytime and feel that they're on their way to the graveyard. But the shift presented opportunity for overtime work at an increased rate of pay and Daddy took the job, probably because our family living expenses had increased with the move to Madisonville. If he considered it a sacrifice, he gave no such indication.

With the mine now running seven days a week and Daddy asleep at church time, the rest of us went to church without him. And since we had to walk because Mother didn't drive, we went to the nearest church: First Baptist.

One Sunday morning, the Cherub Choir marched up on the platform in little white robes with huge red bows tied underneath their chins. "Jesus Loves Me," sang the childish voices. Bright faces glowing, the children's song was even sweeter because some of the voices were off pitch.

Suddenly, I got it. *Jesus loves me!*

At the end of the service, the pastor invited people who wanted to become a Christian to walk up front and speak to him. I felt very much that I wanted to respond, but I couldn't get up the nerve. It was a big church and lots of people were there, as many as five or six hundred, and I was a new girl at church as well as at school.

But that afternoon at home I couldn't let go of the idea, and I finally approached Mother. Whatever our problems the year before, I knew that when I really needed her, she'd be there. "Will you go with me to church tonight so I can join?" *I can do it tonight; fewer people will be there than this mornin'.*

I still remember the click of Mother's high-heeled sandals on the sidewalk as we walked the eight blocks to church that night, and I still remember my pounding heart as I walked up the aisle to the front when the pastor gave the invitation. I was a little frightened of the rotund preacher with the big booming voice, but his eyes were kind and he knew just how to handle my trepidation.

Gently putting one arm around my shoulders, he bent down and whispered a question in my ear. "Yes," I nodded, "I trust Jesus." The pastor said a quiet prayer, and when the congregation finished the hymn, he turned me around to face them. Introducing me, he said he would talk with my parents about baptizing me within the next couple of weeks. *This is really important, everybody, I mean really important. Do you know how important this is? I must look different now. Do I look different? Or do I just feel different? I feel bigger inside, lighter somehow. Ooo, this is big, really big!*

It wasn't like the time with the radio preacher. That time, it was a head level external scheme to get out of trouble. This time, it was a heart level internal response to the truth. *God loves me. I mean, God loves me!*

It was a defining moment, the first step of a fledgling faith.

Hidden Secret

It was a cedar chest day. I still didn't know where Mother kept the key, but now I knew that she enjoyed showing me her keepsakes as much as I enjoyed seeing them. This time, there were some new things—or at least, things new to me.

The wee gold heart dented in the center on both sides and hanging from a broken chain was my baby locket, and the dents were my teething prints. The tiny white satin box lined with green velvet had once contained Mother's wedding band. A few shiny brown buckeyes were souvenirs from one of Daddy's crew members who had returned from a trip to Ohio.

"What's that book over there in the corner?" I asked, pointing to the white cover with black lettering.

"Nothin'," said Mother, sliding the picture album over on top of the book. *Nothin', huh! It's not nothin' if it's in the cedar chest with all your important things!* I had already seen the book, and very clearly. And I was certain beyond all doubt: the word "sex" was in the title.

It was a tricky situation, but I was up to it. Mother didn't want me to know she had a book about sex in the cedar chest, so I pretended I didn't know.

But I *did* know. If Mother had a book about sex in the cedar chest, sex was very important.

Promise of the Future

"Pretty soon," said Mother, "you may not get to go to the movies as often. When you turn 12, you'll have to start payin' full price, just like John does." Mother and I had abandoned the hot house that

187

evening for the front porch swing, the scent of the lilacs on the bush outside my bedroom window gracing the soft summer breeze.

"Lotsa kids just keep payin' half price until they get caught."

"Well, you're not 'lotsa kids,'" said Mother sternly, the metal chains of the swing squeaking in the hooks bolted to the ceiling. "That's cheatin', just as sure as if you put your hand in the cashier's drawer and stole the money. And in our family, we don't cheat. People teach their kids not to lie and steal, but they let them go to movies for half price after they turn 12. And then, when the kids grow up lyin' and stealin', the parents wonder why. Because the parents taught 'em to, that's why!" *Okay, okay!*

The next time John and I went to a movie, I blithely stepped up to the ticket window. I had thought about the occasion for two long weeks and had practiced saying the words, just waiting for the day. "Adult, please," I said, pretending that I was too sophisticated to be impressed with my change in status.

But an even more significant change occurred a few months later. Giving in to the mild but unfamiliar pain in my lower back, I shinnied down the backyard apple tree where I had been daydreaming and went inside the house. When I checked, sure enough, it was my time, the time every preteen girl looks forward to with a mixture of anticipation and dread.

"Time to stop climbin' trees, honey," said Mother, her whistle trailing off and her eyes misting up. "You're a woman now."

It was an exaggeration, and even then I knew it—a teasing recognition that I was growing up. But today, I know something else. I know it was a small letting go, a small admission of our changing relationship, a proud if reluctant acknowledgment of a passage too significant to ignore and too loaded with emotion to give more than a light touch.

It was a promise of the future.

Epilogue: Rainbow Passing

I see the rainbow in the sky, the dew upon the grass;
I see them and I ask not why they glimmer as they
pass. . .[9]

– Walter Savage Landor

Rainbow in the Cedar Chest – II

"Ready?" John's voice sounded distant.

It's my cedar chest. All my most important things are in here. Nobody gets to see inside my cedar chest unless I say, Mother's voice echoed inside my head. But she had given her permission, so I nodded.

We already had our collection of Daddy's things. In his office, John displayed Daddy's safety lantern and hard cap, the black one that had replaced the red one after a falling rock cracked the red one down the middle, leaving Daddy with only a temporary headache and a scratch on his head. And in my home, I displayed his aluminum lunch bucket, the dented and faithful companion that had accompanied him to the mine every day and returned home with him every night.

John raised the lid of the cedar chest and I felt my anticipation rise. Forget the brush of butterfly wings in my stomach; this was the blitz of eagle wings on my soul. *She said it herself. It doesn't mean you're not up to it; it just means you care.*

Quietly, John and I parceled out the keepsakes, some to him and some to me. Except for the book on sex, almost everything I had remembered was there, and additional things Mother had added over the years.

A small figurine of a turtle carved out of coal. Mother's green-backed dresser set, the mirror now broken. The report from the standardized test I had taken at the end of the fifth grade—Mrs. Graham must have returned it to Mother and she had never told me. A small box holding metal bands and wires, the remainders of the orthodontic braces I had worn in the sixth and seventh grades. Certificates for every academic and extracurricular award John and I had ever earned. Invitations to our high school graduations. An invitation to John's college graduation. An invitation to his seminary graduation. A program of his ordination to the ministry. A copy of an article I had published. Invitations to our weddings. Birth announcements of our children. Every birthday and Mother's Day card our children had ever sent her.

A typewritten letter of recommendation from West Kentucky Coal Company dated February 17, 1964: "Samuel Sterling Harris is . . . a good, reliable, conscientious worker and has a thorough knowledge of coal mining . . ." A cassette tape labeled 1979, a scratchy recording of Daddy playing his fiddle. An undated prayer in Mother's handwriting on the back of a used envelope: "Father, thank you for your goodness and mercy. Help me not to be a cantankerous old woman, but one grateful to those who take care of me . . . Amen. Mary Sisk Harris."

St. Paul talked about becoming an adult and seeing the same things he had seen as a child, but seeing them differently. I think I know what he meant. When I was a child, I saw Mother's things, but when I became an adult, I saw what they represented: birth, death, growth, triumph, faith, family, love—Mother's most important things.

The irony of insight is that it takes so long for it to come so quickly. *Hope—it was hope! That's why they never gave up, no matter what the obstacle—meager income, limited education, fear of the coal mine. Love was their motive, yes, but hope was their fuel. They didn't just talk about the lesson of the rainbow, they lived it. It was hope in the future that fueled their purpose of providing more opportunity for John and me than they themselves had. And it was hope in the future that powered Mother's drive to save the family keepsakes and stoked Daddy's resolve to confront his fear of the coal mine so he could support our family. Mother's keepsakes and Daddy's refusal to say goodbye were their rainbows—their signs of hope in the future.*

As the rainbow passes, so eventually did Mother. The cedar chest now abides in my home, the things in it no longer mysterious, no longer hidden, no longer imaginary—Mother's most important things with some of mine added.

Today I showed them to my daughter.

Notes

[1] William Sharp, "The Rose of Flame," in *The Oxford Book of English Mystical Verse*, Nicholson & Lee, eds.,1917.

[2] Padraic Colim, "The Irish Mother in the Penal Days," by John Baniam, *Anthology of Irish Verse,* 1922.

[3] David Rosenthal, "Trees Need Not Walk the Earth," in *Anthology of Magazine Verse for 1920,* William Stanley Braithwaite, ed.

[4] Oliver Wendell Holmes, "A Sun-Day Hymn," in *Hymns of the Christian Church, The Harvard Classics*, 1909-14.

[5] Ibid.

[6] D.H. Lawrence, "Amores" in *The Mystic Blue*, 1916.

[7] James Whitcomb Riley, "A Life-Lesson," in *An American Anthology*, Edmund Clarence Stedman, ed., 1900.

[8] D.H. Lawrence, "Morality and the Novel," in *Phoenix: The Posthumous Papers of D.H. Lawrence*, p. 532, Viking Press, 1916.

[9] Walter Savage Landor, "Resignation," in *The Oxford Book of English Verse,* Arthur Quiller-Couch, ed., 1919.

Printed in the United States
26905LVS00001B/550-552